Germaine Greer

Germaine Greer is one of the most enduring and influential figures of the second wave of the women's movement. *The Female Eunuch* (1970) is one of second-wave feminism's most widely recognised publications, and its author has come to embody and indeed expand our understanding of second-wave feminism in a way that few others have. Yet, while Greer's public visibility never seems to wane, her writings and her politics have failed to attract the kind of sustained critical engagement they warrant. This volume represents the first collection of essays to examine Greer, her politics, her writing, and her status as a feminist celebrity. The essays in this collection cover *The Female Eunuch* (1970), Greer's public rivalry with Arianna Stassinopoulos, her time in America, her ideas and politics, and her styling as feminist fashion icon. Many essays include new insights drawn from previously unseen material in the recently launched Germaine Greer Archive at the University of Melbourne, Australia.

This book was originally published as a special issue of *Australian Feminist Studies*.

Maryanne Dever is a Professor and the Associate Dean in the Faculty of Arts and Social Sciences at the University of Technology Sydney, Australia. She is the joint Editor-in-Chief of *Australian Feminist Studies*.

Anthea Taylor is a Senior Lecturer in the Department of Gender and Cultural Studies at the University of Sydney, Australia. She is the author of three books, including *Celebrity and the Feminist Blockbuster* (2016). Her next book is on Germaine Greer, celebrity, and popular feminism.

Lisa Adkins is a Professor of Sociology and the Head of the School of Social and Political Sciences in the Faculty of Arts and Social Sciences at the University of Sydney, Australia and Academy of Finland Distinguished Professor (2015–19). She is the joint Editor-in-Chief of *Australian Feminist Studies*.

Germaine Greer
Essays on a Feminist Figure

Edited by
**Maryanne Dever, Anthea Taylor
and Lisa Adkins**

LONDON AND NEW YORK

First published 2019
by Routledge
2 Park Square, Milton Park, Abingdon, Oxon, OX14 4RN, UK

and by Routledge
711 Third Avenue, New York, NY 10017, USA

Routledge is an imprint of the Taylor & Francis Group, an informa business

© 2019 Taylor & Francis

All rights reserved. No part of this book may be reprinted or reproduced or utilised in any form or by any electronic, mechanical, or other means, now known or hereafter invented, including photocopying and recording, or in any information storage or retrieval system, without permission in writing from the publishers.

Trademark notice: Product or corporate names may be trademarks or registered trademarks, and are used only for identification and explanation without intent to infringe.

British Library Cataloguing-in-Publication Data
A catalogue record for this book is available from the British Library

ISBN13: 978-1-138-33722-0

Typeset in Myriad Pro
by codeMantra

Publisher's Note
The publisher accepts responsibility for any inconsistencies that may have arisen during the conversion of this book from journal articles to book chapters, namely the possible inclusion of journal terminology.

Disclaimer
Every effort has been made to contact copyright holders for their permission to reprint material in this book. The publishers would be grateful to hear from any copyright holder who is not here acknowledged and will undertake to rectify any errors or omissions in future editions of this book.

Contents

Citation Information vi
Notes on Contributors viii

Introduction – Greer now: editorial 1
Anthea Taylor with Maryanne Dever and Lisa Adkins

1 'Revolution for the hell of it': the transatlantic genesis and serial
   provocations of *The Female Eunuch* 7
   Marilyn Lake

2 The record keeper 22
   Rachel Buchanan

3 Resurrecting Germaine's theory of cuntpower 28
   Megan Le Masurier

4 Germaine Greer's 'arch enemy': Arianna Stassinopoulos'
   1974 Australian tour 43
   Isobelle Barrett Meyering

5 'If we had more like her we would no longer be the unheard
   majority': Germaine Greer's reception in the United States 62
   Rebecca J. Sheehan

6 A feminist fashion icon: Germaine Greer's paisley coat 78
   Petra Mosmann

7 The second best bed, or the female unique? Germaine Greer's unlikely
   championing of love and marriage in *Shakespeare's Wife* 95
   Donald McManus

Index 109

Citation Information

The chapters in this book were originally published in the journal *Australian Feminist Studies*, volume 31, issue 87 (March 2016). When citing this material, please use the original page numbering for each article, as follows:

Introduction
Greer now: editorial
Anthea Taylor with Maryanne Dever and Lisa Adkins
Australian Feminist Studies, volume 31, issue 87 (March 2016) pp. 1–6

Chapter 1
'Revolution for the hell of it': the transatlantic genesis and serial provocations of The Female Eunuch
Marilyn Lake
Australian Feminist Studies, volume 31, issue 87 (March 2016) pp. 7–21

Chapter 2
The record keeper
Rachel Buchanan
Australian Feminist Studies, volume 31, issue 87 (March 2016) pp. 22–27

Chapter 3
Resurrecting Germaine's theory of cuntpower
Megan Le Masurier
Australian Feminist Studies, volume 31, issue 87 (March 2016) pp. 28–42

Chapter 4
Germaine Greer's 'arch enemy': Arianna Stassinopoulos' 1974 Australian tour
Isobelle Barrett Meyering
Australian Feminist Studies, volume 31, issue 87 (March 2016) pp. 43–61

Chapter 5
'If we had more like her we would no longer be the unheard majority': Germaine Greer's reception in the United States
Rebecca J. Sheehan
Australian Feminist Studies, volume 31, issue 87 (March 2016) pp. 62–77

CITATION INFORMATION

Chapter 6
A feminist fashion icon: Germaine Greer's paisley coat
Petra Mosmann
Australian Feminist Studies, volume 31, issue 87 (March 2016) pp. 78–94

Chapter 7
The second best bed, or the female unique? Germaine Greer's unlikely championing of love and marriage in Shakespeare's Wife
Donald McManus
Australian Feminist Studies, volume 31, issue 87 (March 2016) pp. 95–108

For any permission-related enquiries please visit:
http://www.tandfonline.com/page/help/permissions

Notes on Contributors

Lisa Adkins is a Professor of Sociology and the Head of the School of Social and Political Sciences in the Faculty of Arts and Social Sciences at the University of Sydney, Australia and Academy of Finland Distinguished Professor (2015–19). She is the joint Editor-in-Chief of *Australian Feminist Studies*.

Isobelle Barrett Meyering is a Research Fellow at Macquarie University, Sydney, Australia. She has taught in a range of history units at the University of New South Wales, Sydney, Australia, and she also worked as a Research Assistant at the Australian Domestic and Family Violence Clearinghouse from 2009 to 2013.

Rachel Buchanan was the Curator of the Germaine Greer Archive at the University of Melbourne Archives, Australia from October 2015 until March 2018. She is the author of *Stop Press: The Last Days of Newspapers* (2013) and *The Parihaka Album: Lest We Forget* (2010).

Maryanne Dever is a Professor and the Associate Dean in the Faculty of Arts and Social Sciences at the University of Technology Sydney, Australia. She is the joint Editor-in-Chief of *Australian Feminist Studies*.

Marilyn Lake is a Professor in History and Philosophical Studies at the University of Melbourne, Australia. She has published widely on local and international campaigns for sexual and racial equality, citizenship and nationalism, settler colonialism, and the impact of war.

Megan Le Masurier is a Senior Lecturer in the Department of Media and Communications at the University of Sydney, Australia. Her research interests at present are in magazine studies, independent magazines, slow journalism, slow magazines, and popular feminism.

Donald McManus is an Associate Professor at Emory University, Atlanta, USA. His research interests include comedy, popular entertainment, and clown. His articles have appeared in many publications including *The Routledge Companion to Actors' Shakespeare* and *The Routledge Companion to Directors' Shakespeare*.

Petra Mosmann is a Doctoral Candidate in the School of History and International Relations at Flinders University, Adelaide, Australia. Her research explores the relationship between Australian feminist collection practices and histories.

Rebecca J. Sheehan is an Honorary Associate at the United States Studies Centre at the University of Sydney, Australia and a Lecturer in the Sociology of Gender at Macquarie

University, Sydney, Australia. Her work explores the intersections and interactions of identity formations in popular cultures.

Anthea Taylor is a Senior Lecturer in the Department of Gender and Cultural Studies at the University of Sydney, Australia. She is the author of three books, including *Celebrity and the Feminist Blockbuster* (2016). Her next book is on Germaine Greer, celebrity, and popular feminism.

INTRODUCTION
Greer now: editorial

Anthea Taylor with Maryanne Dever and Lisa Adkins

Germaine Greer is undoubtedly one of the West's most iconic feminists, and her public visibility never seems to wane. Over many decades she has worked actively to shape the public meanings that accrue to feminism. The academy, however, has always had an ambivalent relation to Greer – especially in light of her status as a star feminist author. While many feminist critics have sought to destabilise the troublesome academic–popular binary which privileges the former as the more 'authentic' form of feminism, the lack of a sustained critical engagement with Greer reveals that it persists. Even in Australia, Greer's immense contribution to feminist thought is rarely situated within academic scholarship. Not only is it uncommon for undergraduate students to be given Greer's work on survey courses on feminist theory but there have been surprisingly few critical studies of *The Female Eunuch* let alone her subsequent publications.[1] Yet *The Female Eunuch* is one of second-wave feminism's most widely consumed publications, and its celebrity author has come to embody and indeed expand our understanding of second-wave feminism in a way that few others have. The lack of critical attention to this work and its author is even more remarkable, given that research seeking to explore women's understandings of modern feminism has shown that Greer has played a pivotal role, with interviewees often seeing her as synonymous with the second wave (Bulbeck 1997; Dux and Simic 2008). Similarly, letters received by Greer from readers of *The Female Eunuch* make clear that the book, and the copious media appearances of its author, had a transformative impact on many women. Indeed, the enduring cultural reverberations of Greer and her groundbreaking 'feminist blockbuster'[2] are evident in the articles contained here, with a number being preoccupied with teasing out new understandings of its production and reception.

The Female Eunuch has not been Greer's only substantial contribution, however. A prolific writer, Greer has produced a series of popular and academic works, including *The Obstacle Race* (1979), *Sex and Destiny* (1984), *Daddy, We Hardly Knew You* (1989), *The Change* (1991), *Slip-Shod Sybils: Recognition, Rejection and the Women Poets* (1995), *The Whole Woman* (1999), *The Boy* (2003), *Shakespeare's Wife* (2007), *On Rage* (2008), and most recently, *White Beech* (2013). As these titles suggest, throughout her career she has intervened in, and helped precipitate, public debates well beyond feminism and, as Donald McManus demonstrates in this issue, she also built an academic career based on her initial training as a literary scholar. Nevertheless, it is undoubtedly her status as an iconic feminist that has endured across her entire public career. That is, despite these interventions into other fields such as racial and environmental politics, her celebrity capital remains tied to her feminism and especially to her initial 'blockbuster' (Taylor in forthcoming). Her feminist bestseller ensured her a lifelong platform to help inform how feminism comes to mean publicly, a situation Greer exploits with gusto.

Although her proclamation at the beginning of *The Female Eunuch* that 'this book is part of the second feminist wave' (1970, 13) seeks to locate it firmly in the emergent women's liberation movements, its positioning therein was less assured. As Christine Wallace notes in her controversial unauthorised biography, it appeared that 'the less a woman had to do with the women's movement at the time, the more likely it seemed she was to like *The Female Eunuch*' (1997, 206). Despite Greer having little association with the Australian, UK or US women's liberation movements, when the book was published the media in all these contexts nonetheless embarked on a process of 'canonisation', positioning her as the 'epitome of the liberated woman' (Murray 2004, 198) advocated by her book. However, such an assumption of media 'canonisation' fails to take adequate account of Greer's own strategic efforts at persona-building and media intervention, across a number of decades, where she has been active not just as a media source but as a key journalistic actor and highly sought after television performer (Taylor 2014; see also Lilburn et al, 2000). The example of Greer, in particular, allows us to continue the work of refiguring the relationship between second-wave feminism and the mediasphere (Baker-Plummer 2010; Dow 2014; Taylor forthcoming), further complicating 'the established narrative' which contends that the mainstream 'media functioned primarily as feminism's enemy and not its ally in its early period' (Dow 2014, 4). As Rebecca Sheehan demonstrates here, contra these critical narratives regarding inherent hostility towards second-wave feminism, media – and especially audience – response to Greer in the wake of *The Female Eunuch*'s publication was overwhelmingly sympathetic (see also Barrett Meyering here). Similarly, Megan Le Masurier's article maps the importance of Greer's theory of 'cunt power' and its wider media circulation in accessing readers who may not have otherwise been engaged with the burgeoning second wave. In addition to helping refigure these critical narratives about the mediatisation of the second wave, it is also apt that we shift our critical focus towards Greer in a climate where the public meanings given to feminism are increasingly tethered to a neoliberal corporate agenda (Fraser 2013a; Gill and Orgad 2015).

Despite the heterogeneity of the women's movement in the West, liberal feminism often commonly stands in metonymically for the second wave, especially in the mediasphere, with equality discourses displacing more radical formulations. However, recently scholars have turned their attention to radical forms of feminism and how they might be reconceptualised, and perhaps even reanimated (Eichhorn 2015; Hesford 2013; Lusty forthcoming). Kate Eichorn endorses this reconceptualisation, suggesting 'we might begin to understand second wave feminism, even the abandoned utopian project of radical feminism, not as a failed project but rather as the grounds for a feminist project not yet realised' (2015, 254). We would argue that this is a critical project to which 'Greer studies' can make a significant contribution. While Greer may not have had an untroubled relationship with the more radical segments of the women's liberation movement, her politics have never aligned with the 'equality' project that continues to dominate much contemporary public discourse (as per Sheryl Sandberg's [2013] *Lean In*). As Greer remarked recently, 'I'm a liberation feminist, not an equality feminist. Equality is a profoundly conservative aim and it won't achieve anything' (Denham 2015). Liberation feminism is the feminism of *The Female Eunuch*, one that Greer has continued to espouse ever since. It is a feminism that is arguably becoming more vital, useful, and timely than ever, as neoliberalism seems to be recruiting feminism for its own purposes, reducing it to an individualistic project centred on the 'empowerment' of the most privileged of women (Fraser 2013b; McRobbie 2013). This is not to suggest that Greer's feminism should be celebrated uncritically, however. Greer has always been, and remains, a contentious figure for feminism, as her most recent comments concerning transgender women indicate. But given that she continues to inform popular understandings of feminism, an assessment of Greer's wider cultural impact is long overdue and the opening of her archive provides new possibilities for feminist scholars to do just that.

In October 2013, the University of Melbourne announced that it had purchased Germaine Greer's personal papers, reportedly totalling 150 filing cabinets worth of drafts, notes, personal letters, memorabilia and media coverage. The acquisition of this material opens out novel ways to consider Greer's immense contribution to intellectual life, cultural history and public debate in Australia and beyond. As Melbourne University archivist Katrina Dean notes (2013), 'Greer's extraordinary archive is a biography of social and intellectual challenge and change' (see also Buchanan here). Indicative of Greer's ongoing cultural currency, even the University of Melbourne's purchase of the archive itself received extensive media coverage (Gough 2013; Simons 2013). The acquisition of this archive provides a unique opportunity to revisit this iconic figure and her enduring cultural and political impact. In this vein, a number of articles in this special issue have drawn upon archival material to provide new insights into the genesis of *The Female Eunuch* (Lake); audience response to her media appearances on US television (Sheehan); and photographic images and how they were used to shape a particular Greer (Mosmann).

The arrival of Greer's extensive archive coincides with growing critical interest in questions concerning the archiving of different aspects of feminist movements globally and what it might mean more generally for us to 'archive feminism'. In contrast to a number of other Western nations,[3] Australia has no national level collection or repository dedicated to its women's movement. The documentary heritage of Australia's second wave is preserved in a largely ad hoc and geographically dispersed fashion.[4] This invariably limits scholars' access to materials that are central to the project of contesting how the second-wave movement in its national (and international) dimensions is remembered, documented and debated. The records that have most to tell us about informal political movements are generally those retained in the first instance by individuals rather than by institutions and the women's movement is no different as Greer's collection demonstrates. However, as the second-wave activist community ages we confront the challenge that many of their unique collections of records face somewhat uncertain futures as these women retire, downsize, and become increasingly frail. But potential archival loss is only one of the challenges that must be acknowledged. Even where we have them, records do not speak for themselves and feminist scholars are increasingly stressing the manner in which all archives are 'figured' (Stoler 2009), that is, enmeshed in histories and politics that must be accounted for before any investigation of individual collections can proceed. This complicates how we approach collections such as Greer's as the conditions of collecting, acquiring, processing and displaying materials must also form part of our engagements. In this sense, Greer's archive cannot be looked upon simply as a repository of interesting but inert documents awaiting our scholarly gaze; the collection will always be entangled in wider questions concerning the politics of knowledge, particular forms of privilege, and the making and unmaking of feminist memories.

In producing this themed issue, *Australian Feminist Studies* continues its work of investigating (and troubling) the terms that join together feminism as a political project, feminism as an intellectual project, and feminist activism as they are folded into contemporary social and cultural change. The figure of Germaine Greer highlights for us and for our contributors precisely the complexity of this folding, not least in how Greer troubles distinctions between the academic and the popular, the authentic and the non-authentic, the celebrity and the scholar, history and memory, and the past and the present. Inasmuch as the contributors to this issue necessarily locate the figure of Greer in proximity to the present, they add a new intensity to its significance for feminism's future.

Notes

1. Notable exceptions include Spongberg (1993); Lilburn, Magarey, and Sheridan (2000), which however focus on Greer as a media personality rather than her feminism.
2. This is a term coined by Henderson and Rowlands (1996), and upon which Taylor builds (forthcoming).
3. These include: the Canadian Women's Movement Archive which is housed in the special collections of the University of Ottawa Library (see: http://uottawa.ca.libguides.com/content.php?pid=194014&sid=1626252); and the Netherlands which supports the International Archives for the Women's Movement housed within their Aletta Institute for Women's History in Amsterdam (see: http://wasi.alexanderstreet.com/help/view/the_aletta_institute_in_amsterdam_and_its_international_collections). For further discussion of the Netherlands case, see Ypeij and Wieringa (2009) and De Haan (2004).
4. The collections that exist are partial, geographically dispersed and more often than not they have come into existence (and survived) as a result of the energies of dedicated individuals. They include: the Adelaide Women's Liberation Movement Archive housed in the State Library of South Australia, the Victorian Women's Liberation and Lesbian Feminist Archive also housed by the University of Melbourne Archives, the Jessie Street National Women's Library, and the Lespar Library of Women's Liberation housed within the special collections at Murdoch University. Individual women can be searched via the Australian Women's Archive Project (http://www.womenaustralia.info/awap.html). For detailed analysis of women's movement records in Australian collecting institutions, see Bartlett, Dever, and Henderson (2007). Further records and artifacts concerning Australian second wave activism remain in private hands, although some figures – such as Merle Thornton – have negotiated for their papers ultimately to go to key collecting institutions (see Dever 2014).

Disclosure statement

No potential conflict of interest was reported by the authors.

References

Baker-Plummer, B. 2010. "News and Feminism: A Historic Dialog." *Journalism and Communication Monographs* 12 (3/4): 145–203.
Bartlett, A., M. Dever, and M. Henderson. 2007. "Notes Towards an Archive of Australian Feminist Activism." *Outskirts*, 16. Accessed March 13, 2016. http://www.outskirts.arts.uwa.edu.au/volumes/volume-16/bartlett.
Bulbeck, C. 1997. *Living Feminism: The Impact of the Women's Movement on Three Generations of Australian Women*. Cambridge: Cambridge University Press.
Dean, K. 2013. "Why Greer's Life in Letters is One for the Archives." *The Conversation*. Accessed November 1. https://theconversation.com/why-germaine-greers-life-in-letters-is-one-for-the-archives-19625.
De Haan, F. 2004. "Getting to the Source. A 'Truly International' Archive for the Women's Movement (IAV, now IIAV): From its Foundation in Amsterdam in 1935 to the Return of its Looted Archives in 2003." *Journal of Women's History* 16 (4): 148–172.
Denham, J. 2015. "International Women's Day 2015: Germaine Greer Brands Feminism 'Ageist' and Demands Right to 'Grow Up'." *The Independent*, Accessed March 8. http://www.independent.co.uk/news/people/international-womens-day-2015-germaine-greer-brands-feminism-ageist-and-demands-the-right-to-grow-up-10094000.html.
Dever, M. 2014. "Archiving Feminism: Papers, Politics, Posterity." *Archivaria* 77: 25–42.
Dow, B. 2014. *Watching Women's Liberation, 1970: Feminism's Pivotal Year on the Network News*. Chicago: University of Illinois Press.
Dux, M., and Z. Simic. 2008. *The Great Feminist Denial*. Melbourne: Melbourne University Press.
Eichhorn, K. 2015. "Feminism's There: On Post-Ness and Nostalgia." *Feminist Theory* 16 (3): 251–264.
Fraser, N. 2013a. *Fortunes of Feminism*. London: Verso.
Fraser, N. 2013b. "How Feminism Became Capitalism's Handmaiden." *The Guardian*, Accessed October 14. http://www.theguardian.com/commentisfree/2013/oct/14/feminism-capitalist-handmaiden-neoliberal.
Gill, R., and S. Orgad. 2015. "The Confidence Cult(ure)." *Australian Feminist Studies* 30 (86): 324–344.
Gough, D. 2013. "Germaine Greer Sells Archive to Melbourne University." *The Age*, Accessed October 28. http://www.theage.com.au/victoria/germaine-greer-sells-archive-to-melbourne-university-20131028-2wbho.html.
Greer, G. (1970) 1993. *The Female Eunuch*. Reprint. London: Flamingo.
Greer, G. 1979. *The Obstacle Race: The Fortunes of Women Painters and Their Work*. London: Martin Secker and Warburg.
Greer, G. 1984. *Sex and Destiny: The Politics of Human Fertility*. London: HarperCollins.
Greer, G. 1991. *The Change: Women, Ageing and the Menopause*. London: Hamish Hamilton.
Greer, G. 1989. *Daddy, We Hardly Knew You*. London: Hamish Hamilton.
Greer, G. 1995. *Slip-Shod Sibyls: Recognition, Rejection and the Woman Poet*. London: Viking.
Greer, G. 1999. *The Whole Woman*. London: Doubleday.
Greer, G. 2003. *The Boy*. London: Thames & Hudson.
Greer, G. 2007. *Shakespeare's Wife*. London: Bloomsbury.
Greer, G. 2008. *On Rage*. Carlton, Vic.: Melbourne University Press.
Greer, G. 2013. *White Beech: The Rainforest Years*. London: Bloomsbury.
Henderson, M., and S. Rowlands. 1996. "Damned Bores and Slick Sisters: The Selling of Blockbuster Feminism in Australia." *Australian Feminist Studies* 11 (23): 9–16.

Hesford, V. 2013. *Feeling Women's Liberation*. Durham: Duke University Press.
Lilburn, S., S. Magarey, and S. Sheridan. 2000. "Celebrity Feminism as Synthesis: Germaine Greer, The Whole Woman and the Australian Print Media." *Continuum* 14 (3): 335–348.
Lusty, N. forthcoming. "Riot Grrrl Manifestos and Radical Vernacular Feminism." *Australian Feminist Studies*.
McRobbie, A. 2013. "Feminism, The Family and The New Mediated Maternalism." *New Formations* 80–81: 119–137.
Murray, S. 2004. *Mixed Media: Feminist Presses and Publishing Politics*. London: Pluto.
Sandberg, S. 2013. *Lean In: Women, Work, and The Will to Lead*. London: WH Allen.
Simons, M. 2013. "Germaine Greer Sells Archive to University of Melbourne." *The Guardian*. Accessed October 28 http://www.theguardian.com/books/2013/oct/28/germaine-greer-sells-archive-to-university-of-melbourne.
Spongberg, M. 1993. ""If She's so Great, How Come so Many Pigs Dig Her?": Germaine Greer and the Malestream Press." *Women's History Review* 2 (3): 407–419.
Stoler, A. L. 2009. *Along the Archival Grain*. Princeton: Princeton UP.
Taylor, A. in press. *Celebrity and the Feminist Blockbuster: The Changing Face of Celebrity Feminism*. Basingstoke: Palgrave Macmillan.
Taylor, A. 2014. "Germaine Greer's Adaptable Celebrity: Feminism, Unruliness, and Humour on the British Small Screen." *Feminist Media Studies* 14 (5): 759–774.
Wallace, C. 1997. *Greer: Untamed Shrew*. Sydney: Pan Macmillan.
Ypeij, A., and S Wieringa. 2009. *Traveling Heritages: New Perspectives on Collecting, Preserving and Sharing Women's History*. Amsterdam: Amsterdam University Press.

'Revolution for the hell of it': the transatlantic genesis and serial provocations of *The Female Eunuch*

Marilyn Lake

ABSTRACT

In a synopsis sent to her publisher outlining her plans for a 'sensational' book, Germaine Greer wrote:

> If Eldridge Cleaver can write a book about the frozen soul of the negro, as part of the progress towards a correct statement of the coloured man's problem, a woman must eventually take steps towards delineating the female condition as she finds it scored upon her sensibility. I know myself to be an anomaly, a lucky survival, but men, so is Cleaver: if he is a genius, a criminal, a delinquent only such a person who escapes from the glass mountain can describe it and pass the message on … .

The recent opening of the Greer archive at the University of Melbourne offers researchers new understanding of the transAtlantic orientation of *The Female Eunuch* and the inspirations and models provided by a range of contemporary radical male American writers, notably Eldridge Cleaver, Abbie Hoffman, Jerry Rubin and Norman Mailer. Greer's papers contain pitches to the publisher, numerous drafts and revisions of her book proposal, summaries of the book's contents, clues to its anticipated readers and towards the end of the process, a 'dedication'. Drafts are partly handwritten, partly typed and combinations of these, amended and revised, all evolving, illuminating Greer's chosen genre, discursive frames of reference and the *motif* of castration. The papers provide insight into *The Female Eunuch*'s defining analogy between the condition of woman and that of the 'American Negro' and illuminate media strategies that ensured the book became an iconic feminist text.

Strumpet Voluntary

In an early three-page synopsis for the book that would be called *The Female Eunuch*, Germaine Greer proposed:

> I shall describe some ways of being outrageous which I privately think also mirror some of our deepest desires, so that women can make revolution for the hell of it (my book is aware of Jerry Rubin too) [Jerry Rubin crossed out and replaced by 'Abby [sic] Hoffman'] which is the only kind at all likely to succeed.[1]

Written for her publisher friend, Sonny Mehta, then working at MacGibbon and Kee, later to head up Pan and then Knopf in the United States, Greer's pitch promised a 'sensational' book. *Revolution for the Hell of It*, the book by Abbie Hoffman whose title she quoted in the synopsis was published in 1968. Hoffman was an American anarchist, anti-war activist and member of the 'Chicago Eight' (charged with conspiracy and incitement to riot). Always a 'media junky' in the words of a friend, one of Hoffman's best-known stunts was an invasion of the New York Stock Exchange, where he and his friends threw a fistful of dollars onto the stock exchange floor and watched the traders scramble to pick them up (Jezer 1992, 112). This 'media event', as later described, was screened on television around the world.

Hoffman's *Revolution for the Hell of It* has been described as one of the 'quintessential texts of the era'. According to Raskin:

> No other book—including Norman Mailer's *The Armies of the Night* and Eldridge Cleaver's *Soul on Ice* ... also published in 1968—captured as successfully the frenetic energy and the disjointed character of the times in which it was written. (1996, 174)

In his introduction to Hoffman's *Autobiography*, Mailer, an early influence on Greer, would praise Hoffman as 'a bona fide American revolutionary' (2000, xiii). The call to revolution excited Greer, but in *The Female Eunuch* she would offer a manifesto for a different kind of revolution: 'the cunt must come into its own' (1971a, 318). Mailer was delighted: 'A wind in this prose whistled up the kilts of male conceit' (1971, 43, 48, 50–51).

Until the recent opening of Greer's personal archive, now the property of the University of Melbourne, there was little information on the record about the conception of *The Female Eunuch*, its sources of inspiration, chosen genre, discursive frames of reference and *motif* of castration. Fortunately for historians, Greer's papers contain pitches to the publisher, numerous drafts and revisions of her book proposal, summaries of the book's contents, clues to its anticipated readers and towards the end of the process, a 'dedication'. Drafts are partly handwritten, partly typed and combinations of these, amended and revised, all evolving, indeed 'transmogrified'—to use one of Mailer's favourite words—proposals.

The working drafts—with sentences and phrases struck through and replaced by new thoughts and phrases—now make for interesting reading. It is instructive, for example, to compare the draft 'Summary' with the final version printed at the beginning of *The Female Eunuch*. The draft summary began on a hostile note: 'So far the female liberation movement is tiny, privileged and overrated.'[2] The printed version opens with a rather more conciliatory and inclusive statement: 'This book is part of the second feminist wave' (Greer 1971a, 11). The draft proposals highlight the discursive and cultural contexts in which Greer conceived her book. They also make clear that the authors to whom she looked for inspiration and whom she cited as authorities were radical American admirers of Black urban machismo: Norman Mailer, Eldridge Cleaver, Abbie Hoffman and Jerry Rubin.

In this article, I suggest that a reading of Greer's pitch to the publisher and early draft proposals throws new light on the book's early American orientations, its masculine identifications and Greer's analogy between the condition of women and the American 'Negro'. The drafts also anticipate the crucial role media visibility would play in Greer's (self) marketing and writing strategy. She noticed (and seemed bothered by) the fact that the burgeoning women's movement in the United States was 'a hot number', attracting considerable publicity (Greer 1986a, 25–29). She referred especially to the attention given to SCUM (Society for Cutting Up Men), WITCH and Valerie Solanas (Greer 1986a, 25–27). In the draft 'Summary', she noted that Betty Friedan had been 'given massive coverage by the press and television'.[3] In other words the women's movement was news. As

Jerry Rubin, American counter-cultural icon and anti-war activist (quoted by Greer) wrote in *DO IT! Scenarios of the Revolution*, 'the media does not report "news" it creates it. An event happens when it goes on TV and becomes a myth' (Albert and Albert 1984, 443). In 1970, Germaine Greer published an outrageous book, went on TV and became a 'media freak', in her words. Her book entered mythology as the kind that 'changed women's lives' in testimonies often penned long after the event (Bulbeck 1997; Adelaide 1998, 12; McGrath 1999). 'Her ideas freed a generation of women, me included', wrote novelist Kate Grenville, in 2009 (10). 'It blew my mind and shaped the course of my life', testified journalist Maggie Alderson, in 2012 (Alderson 2012, 6).

When Greer first began to think about writing a book, in 1969, one of the titles she chose was 'Strumpet Voluntary'. She liked sex. All women should enjoy sex. The problem was, she told a journalist, that 'women have somehow been separated from their libido, from their faculty of desire, from their sexuality' (Weintraub 1971). In a handwritten note, contained in papers later labelled 'TFE: editorial', Greer noted '21 April 1969' as the 'day on which my book begins itself, and Janis Joplin sings at Albert Hall. Yesterday the title was Strumpet Voluntary—what shall it be today?' In her pitch to her publisher, contained in the same papers, Greer explained 'why I think this book should be written, which is the same as explaining why I should write it':

> Firstly I suppose it is to expiate my guilt at being an uncle Tom to my sex. I don't like women. I probably share in all the effortless and unconscious contempt that men pour on women. Probably—I do .... Most women would deny that they are oppressed, which is why it will prove harder to liberate them that it was to liberate the *soul* of the negro ... [4]

In a later draft proposal, Greer advised that what she intended in writing a book about women—'for which I have not yet devised a title'—was a 'collection of essays about what it is to be a woman in 1969. The aim is not to present a plan, or even a series of certainties or correct observations, but a correct statement of a problem'.[5] Then followed a summary of her goal. 'My object in all this', she wrote,

> is not to separate women from men, but to ally them in a different way, so that instead of the mutually limiting relationship ['of dependant and provider' replaced by 'which is not only financial' and replaced again by 'interlocking dependencies'] there is spontaneous self-generating attachment, which is among other things more sexual than at present.

['I want to make women more attractive to men, for longer. My flag reads "Better orgasms for all"'—these sentences later crossed out.][6]

In successive proposals, Greer promised her publisher that she would not produce an academic work. Rather it would be a 'sensational book'. Her pitch followed a conversation in which Greer and Mehta had discussed contemporary radical writing in the United States:

> It will therefore be a sensational book. I shall strive to write with the fullness of my femaleness, in a language both accurate and sensuous, a ['powerful' added] direct rhetoric ['as powerful as Eldrige Cleaver's' crossed out], ['speaking to' replaced by 'aimed at'] the viscera of womankind, not the babble of bluestockings. ['jargon' crossed out]. I hope to preserve my creative rage through the writing of this book, ['in another of Mailer's passages, transmogrified' crossed out], that though the shits are killing us, we have not died.[7]

The Female Eunuch was published in London in October 1970. It was not born a feminist book, but it became one, in dynamic and transformative encounters with the emerging women's liberation movement and modern mass media. The first publications to emerge from the movement itself, pointedly dedicated to the spirit of 'sisterhood' had appeared two years earlier in New York, a city Greer first visited in 1968, before she considered writing a book of her own (Wallace 1997, 211). The 'SCUM manifesto' was dated 1967–1968. 'Notes from the First Year' appeared in 1968 (Morgan 1970; Tanner 1971). Within months of *The Female Eunuch*'s American publication by McGraw-Hill, in 1971, followed by a book tour ('interviews, television, parties and book signings in American cities, all the way from New York to San Francisco and back'), *The Female Eunuch* was transformed into a best-selling, iconic, transnational text for the times (Roxon 1971, 7).

Much has been written about the media's fevered embrace of the author and the book: the excited response of male and female journalists, magazine editors, columnists, television producers and feminist critics, its widespread impact in Britain, the United States and Australia, and the many translations that followed. As biographer Christine Wallace put it, *The Female Eunuch* became 'feminism's smash-hit book' (Wallace 1997, 190). Greer became a 'media star', a 'megastar', the toast of the talk shows, an instant celebrity, or, in the words of women's studies scholars, 'a feminist pioneer in the celebrity zone' (Spongberg 1993; Lilburn, Magarey, and Sheridan 2000, 335).

Greer as outsider

In this article, I draw on the Greer papers to highlight the importance of the transAtlantic discursive and publishing context to the initial conception of *The Female Eunuch*. Although Greer had completed her Ph.D. degree at the University of Cambridge, and worked in London, her book was not a product of the English women's movement, whose leading activists were keen to distance themselves, rejecting Greer as an outsider, an egotist and 'heterosexual chauvinist' (Coote and Campbell 1987, 240–241; Segal 1987, 88; Wandor 1990). 'All Germaine Greer's comments on women's liberation both in England and America have an external quality', remarked historian Sheila Rowbotham. 'They lack both the passion and the self criticism which women who have experienced working within movements write' (Rowbotham 1970, 18).

In her account of the beginnings of the English women's liberation movement, Rowbotham detailed numerous local events, such as the strike at the Ford factory in Dagenham, the formation of grass roots collectives, the establishment of workshops and publication of newsletters (1990, 14–27). The story of the English women's movement usually gave pride of place to the first women's liberation conference, planned in 1969 and held over a weekend at Ruskin College, Oxford, in February 1970, seven months before the publication of *The Female Eunuch*. This legendary gathering of 400 women, 60 children and 40 men was—according to participant Wandor, a vocal critic of Greer, 'a historic moment in post-war British feminism' (1990, 2; Rowbotham 1990, 22). Greer may have talked to 'ordinary little women of all ages' in the 'retrogressive north of England', as she said in the draft 'Summary' of her book, but she had no time for 'professional liberationists', whose concept of liberty was 'vacuous' and whose 'same faces' appeared 'every time a feminist issue was discussed'.[8] In the published 'Summary' in *The Female Eunuch* the 'ordinary little women' had been transformed into 'provincial women decently hatted and dressed' (Greer 1971a, 12). Soon it would be Greer's face that was omnipresent. 'Australia's Miss Greer has become a common face on BBC talk shows' noted the *Washington Post* in April 1971

(Zito 1971). Within months she would be well recognised on American and Australian TV screens as well.

Australian profiles of Greer and *The Female Eunuch* have, not surprisingly, been pleased to cast her as a local girl made good and a prominent example of that Australian institution —the expatriate (Britain 1997; Alomes 1999). Australian writers invariably focussed on Greer's Australianness, growing up in the 1950s suburbs, her unhappy family life, a scholarship girl educated in Melbourne and Sydney, where she joined the libertarian 'Push', her early talent for theatrical performance and subsequent immersion in London's underground culture associated with Richard Neville's *Oz* magazine (Connolly 1970, 21; King 1971, 6; Roxon 1971, 7; Dunstan 2004). Australian historian Bongiorno proposed that *The Female Eunuch* might be best understood as 'one of a series of remarkable books by Australian authors … that helped to define the tone and content … of Anglophone cultural and intellectual life in the 1970s' (2013, 295).

Feminist critics of *The Female Eunuch*, on the other hand, especially American women's liberationists expressed dismay at Greer's lack of solidarity with the international women's movement, her seemingly gratuitous attacks on other women, her dismissal of earlier generations of 'blue-stocking' feminists, her avid heterosexuality, seductive appeal to men ('Saucy feminist that even men like' as the front cover of *Life* magazine described her) and lack of a coherent political program (Dreifus 1971; Reed 1971; Spongberg 1993, 414–416). By contrast, Lesley Tanner's 1970 collection *Voices from Women's Liberation* (dedicated 'To All Sisters') had respectfully paid tribute to, and published the writings of, a number of pioneering feminists such as Mary Wollstonecraft, Sarah Grimke, Harriet Martineau and suffragists, Elizabeth Cady Stanton, Susan B. Anthony, Elizabeth Blackwell and Carrie Chapman Catt. In *The Female Eunuch*, Greer wrote that the 'suffragettes betrayed their own cause and prepared the way for the failure of emancipation' (1971a, 12) American feminist, Evelyn Reed responded in a sharp appraisal in *International Socialist Review*: 'Greer is a model for those men who want more sex and less politics from women in the feminist movement' (1971, 10). Greer was represented as an outsider not only in England, but by the women's movement more generally. She also preferred to cast herself that way: 'I don't belong to anything. My role is simply to preach to the unconverted. I'm the one who talks to *Playboy*' (Greer 1972, 64).

'If Eldridge Cleaver can write a book … '

Aspects of the story of the book's commissioning are well known from Greer's telling of it (1984, 98; Britain 1997, 139). Following the end of Granada TV's Kenny Everett series, *Nice Time*, Greer's agent suggested she write a book to mark the 50th anniversary of the granting of (the first stage of) women's suffrage in the United Kingdom in 1918, perhaps to highlight the limited nature of the suffragettes' achievement. 'My agent wanted me to write about the failure of emancipation', she told Bell in an interview for the *Sydney Morning Herald* in July 1969, 'but I couldn't get even mildly excited about that' (1969, 5).

Shortly afterwards, Sonny Mehta, then working for MacGibbon and Kee (an imprint of Granada Publishing Ltd), persuaded her that she could channel her contempt for the idea of commemorating women's suffrage into 'creative rage'. Greer should write a book about the woeful condition of women in the late 1960s and how they must liberate themselves. For as she insisted in a draft summary, 'demonstrating, compiling reading lists, and sitting on committees are not themselves liberated behaviour'.[9] The distinctive character and main argument of *The Female Eunuch* took shape in dialogue between publisher and author. It had to be a popular book, Mehta insisted, not an academic or scholarly study. Greer was happy to oblige. 'I have abandoned the notion of a systematic study', she wrote, 'for a more organic form .... beginning at the black/white confrontation of male and female in our language and symbolism ... The last chapter will be my apocalypse'.[10]

Although initially a book occasioned by the anniversary of women's suffrage in the United Kingdom, offering a meditation on how women had subsequently used or squandered their newfound electoral power, this would not be a work of history. Greer had no interest or training in history. Her Masters and Ph.D. theses were undertaken in the discipline of English literature and as became well known, her doctoral dissertation, completed at the University of Cambridge in 1967, was on Shakespeare's early comedies. The history of English women's political campaigns and subsequent disappointments excited no curiosity. Nor did she seem aware that Australia—the country of her birth—had led the world in granting full political rights to women in 1902, long before British women's achievement.

In any case, this would be irrelevant, because Greer conceived of her subject not historically, but in existentialist terms, as had her predecessor, Simone de Beauvoir, in *The Second Sex*, published in French in 1949 and in English translation in 1953. For de Beauvoir, the problem of woman was her status as 'Other' ('He is the Subject, he is the Absolute—she is the Other') (1987, 16). In *The Feminine Mystique* published in 1963, Friedan—dismissed by Greer as a reformist and latter-day suffragist—had famously investigated 'the problem that has no name' among educated, but discontented American housewives (1965). In the United Kingdom, Juliet Mitchell published 'Women: The Longest Revolution' in 1966 in *New Left Review*, an essay she elaborated in her scholarly book *Woman's Estate*. In 1970, Shulamith Firestone published *The Dialectic of Sex*. Greer entered the field in the same year, determined to shock and offend: 'The book will draw fire from all the articulate sections of the community.'[11] She defined her subject in universalist terms as the 'problem of female identity'.[12]

The problem that once 'had no name' (as Friedan had put it) she identified as 'the castration of women' (Greer 1971a, 16). When Greer began to think about the problem of 'identity' in a 'White Man's society' she did not turn to other feminist writers or British New Leftists, but contemporary American writers, who addressed in particular the 'problem of the Negro'. 'It is odd', she wrote,

> that the white liberal of 1969 has accepted the idea that negroes, whom he does not know, must free themselves by establishing their own identity, when he would be surprised to hear that the women who live with him are unfree and unrealized. But then, of course, he does not know his woman either.[13]

Soul on Ice was a key inspiration. Written in prison by founding member of the militant Black Panther Party and serial rapist, Eldridge Cleaver, this collection of essays was published in 1968. Introducing the author as one of 'the distinctive new literary voices to be heard in that decade', American literary critic Geismar located *Soul on Ice* in a tradition of great Black writing: 'It has echoes of Richard Wright's *Native Son*, just as its true moral affinity is with one of the few other fine books of our period, the *Autobiography of Malcolm X*' (1968, xi). The Black man's 'soul' had been colonised by the White man (as WEB DuBois had suggested decades before) (Lake and Reynolds 2008, 1). 'We shall have our manhood', cried Cleaver, echoing DuBois. 'We shall have it or the earth will be levelled by our attempts to gain it' (1968, 61).

Like African-Americans, women had to set out a 'statement of their condition', said Greer.

> If Eldridge Cleaver can write a book about the frozen soul of the negro, as part of the progress towards a correct statement of the coloured man's problem, a woman must eventually ['come to write' deleted] take steps towards delineating the female condition as she finds it scored upon her sensibility.

In the midst of this hand written passage, Greer wrote between the lines another unfinished sentence that trailed off: 'It is one of the anomalies of 1969 that while the equality and the oppression of the negro are if not ["seminal"?] .... .'[14]

By then a lecturer in English at Warwick University, Greer was a high-achieving academic. She wondered whether her exceptional status might be thought to disqualify her from writing about ordinary women, but reassured herself that 'I am probably as fit to do this as any negro leader.' Maybe she was 'an anomaly, a lucky survival, ["but men so is Cleaver: he is a genius and a criminal, a delinquent"—crossed out] but only such a person, a person who escapes from the glass mountain can describe it and pass the message on'. She had come to

> a point in her own travailed life when I must ['write my sisters a book'—crossed out] speak, and what I speak, in all its confusion, is my book, which could be called The Female Eunuch or why I ['despise/hate/dislike'] women.[15]

The draft proposals for The Female Eunuch are full of angry diatribes about ordinary women and the compromises they were prepared to make, attacks on the 'female parasite', the 'married woman' and the 'working wife', who combined family life and paid work, who rushed away from work at lunchtime to buy the dinner, and mothers, who falsely claimed to find fulfilment in raising children. 'Any moron can bring up kids, well or badly, somehow. The most intelligent, resourceful woman can expect no greater measure of success and justification than the moron.' Women should face up to the truth of their situation. 'Women are such liars, such face-savers, that they pretend, at all points along their experience, to be gratified, peaceful, satisfied when they AIN'T.' Men needed to be freed from such miserable companions. ['What husband coming home from a hard day at the office wants to be met by a wife with grievances, boredoms'—a sentence later deleted].[16]

In one handwritten passage of her draft synopsis, Greer emphasised that her 'case rests upon no misanthropy. Indeed my problem is much more that I cannot like women'. Like Mary Wollstonecraft and Simone de Beauvoir before her, Greer was frustrated and impatient with women, indignant at their 'bad faith', as de Beauvoir termed it, their complicity with men and refusal to take on the responsibility of freedom:

> Man struggles to be free of us, and we cling on, terrified to drop into the void, distrustful of our own capabilities, afraid ['perhaps'—deleted] of freedom, because it is the most demanding condition .... I would have woman release her last clutch at man, not to have her retreat into some absurd Amazonian society, but to improve female congress with the male .... .[17]

Greer wanted to write a book that would show women how their 'psychic energy' could be released into real creativity, just as the 'Negro' also needed to be free.[18]

The 'Negro' was 'hip' and a source of inspiration for 'hipsters'. In 1957, Mailer had written what became a cult essay on 'Hip' culture that he called 'The White Negro', subtitled 'Superficial Reflections on the Hipster', in which he suggested that 'the source of Hip [was] the negro' who lived on 'the margin between totalitarianism and democracy for two centuries' (Mailer 1957). 'The Negro', wrote Mailer, 'had the simplest of alternatives: live a life of constant humility or ever-threatening danger'. In this light the New York 'hipster ... could be considered a white negro'. Their existential condition was the same as 'the psychopath' and 'the saint and the bullfighter and lover'. Mailer's essay dwelt at length on 'the search after a good orgasm' and the 'energy, life, sex, force' that explained 'the psychopathic element of hip', 'the hipster's desire for absolute sexual freedom' (1957). In place of class conflict as the driving force of historical change, Mailer posited the dynamic role of the struggle between revolution and conformity. Greer would join that struggle.

Abbie Hoffman had claimed that 'The White Negro' was influential in his turn to political rebellion. For him, as for Mailer, the Negro was a favourite 'identity model' (Jezer 1992, 29–30). Another reader who became a great admirer, indeed a self-styled 'student' of 'The White Negro' was Cleaver, who according to Michele Wallace 'did a lot to politicize sexuality in the Black movement' (1968, 98; Wallace 1979, 66). Cleaver reported that he practised raping black women, before crossing the tracks to prey on white women (1968, 14). Rape was not a crime against women, in this scenario, but 'an insurrectionary act', a revolutionary political act (Cleaver 1968, 14).

Cleaver argued that the white man had deprived the black man of his masculinity, his energy and his virility. He had 'castrated him in the center of his burning skull' (Cleaver 1968, 103). Greer would appropriate Cleaver's argument about the castration of Black men to develop her argument in *The Female Eunuch*, citing in a break-out quote a passage from 'The Allegory of the Black Eunuchs':

> The myth of the strong black woman is the other side of the coin of the myth of the beautiful dumb blonde. The white man turned the white woman into a weak-minded, weak-bodied, delicate freak, a sex pot, and placed her on a pedestal; he turned the black woman into a strong self-reliant Amazon and deposited her in his kitchen ... The white man turned himself into the Omnipotent Administrator and established himself in the Front Office. (1971a, 59)

Significantly, however, Greer omitted a key phrase. The ellipsis repressed the specificity of the Black woman's position in Cleaver's analysis. Cleaver had actually written of the white man that 'he turned the black woman into a strong self-reliant Amazon and deposited her in his kitchen—the secret of Aunt Jemima's bandanna' (1968, 162).

In her universalising of the female condition, Greer repressed a key aspect of Cleaver's analysis, which was the privileged situation of the white woman compared to the black woman. Cleaver had agonised over his desire for white women and finally identified it as an effect of the racist work of the white man, whom he called the Omnipotent Administrator. 'The elite woman thus becomes the Ultrafeminine', he wrote, 'while the woman below becomes Subfeminine'. Greer's argument in *The Female Eunuch* ignored Cleaver's racial differentiations. Inspired by his analysis of the 'Negro soul', Greer could admit no racial dimension to femininity. For her the white woman was identified with both the kitchen and the 'Ultrafeminine' and thus universalised as the 'Eternal Feminine'

(Greer 1971a, 15). In *The Female Eunuch*, the woman's essential quality, like that of the Black man, was her 'castratedness'. Was the white woman also a type of 'white negro'?

Significantly, Greer chose not to adopt the corollary of Cleaver's argument in *Soul on Ice*, his suggestion, directed at James Baldwin, that when a Black man had sex with the 'Omnipotent Administrator', he became a traitor, because he 'focussed on "whiteness" all the love in his pent up soul' (1968, 103). Greer seemingly never contemplated the possibility that in her enthusiasm for heterosexual intercourse—'embrace and stimulate the penis instead of taking it'—she might be focussing all the love in her own pent up soul on men and masculinity (Greer 1971a, 42). This thought would soon occur to her feminist critics and many male admirers in the mainstream media, including *Life* magazine, *Newsweek* and *Playboy,* to whom she provided a ten-page interview based on five 2-hour taping sessions conducted in Italy over several days (Greer 1972).

'My reporter [like Mailer—deleted] must be my heroine'

Given her feelings of alienation from women in general, Greer explained that the book must, 'in an essential way', be about her own 'sensibility': it was 'the only one she knew [closely'—crossed out] and 'my reporter, ["like Mailer" deleted] must also be my heroine'.[19] In so-called New Journalism, the literary technique of participant observation, wherein the reporter also became the subject of the story had been exemplified in Mailer's acclaimed 1968 essays *Armies of the Night* and *Miami and the Siege of Chicago*. Greer was an admirer of Mailer's writing, especially his 1965 novel *The American Dream*. It was simply philistine; she said in response to Kate Millett's critique in *Sexual Politics* not to recognise what 'a great book' it was. It was a pity that 'Norman Mailer was his own worst enemy … I'd really like to help that man' (Greer 1971b, 1986c; Weintraub 1971).

In the United States, especially, *The Female Eunuch* was received as a siren song to men. Most male profiles of the book proceeded by distinguishing Greer from other—aggressive, unattractive—'women's lib writers' (Korengold 1971, 50). *Newsweek* cast 'the awesome 6-foot figure of 32-year-old Germaine Greer' as 'a dazzling combination of erudition, eccentricity and eroticism whose passionate treatise entitled "The Female Eunuch" may well be women's lib's most realistic—and least anti-male—manifesto'. Comparing her with Kate Millett, Ti-Grace Atkinson and Robin Morgan, journalist Korengold gushed:

> Australian-born and magnetically attractive, she boasts of having spent fourteen years as a 'groupie' follower of pop musicians. To add to her cachet, she looks like a cross between Anna Magnani and Vanessa Redgrave, affects a wildly uninhibited lifestyle with an all-embracing libido … (1971, 50)

It was a surprise and a relief that Greer displayed 'relatively little hostility toward males, and indeed may go over better with men, whom she tends to pity for their obsession with virility'. Even better, she openly admitted to enjoying bedding down with men. 'I don't think the penis is entirely irrelevant, largely because I like men.' At last, 'a woman with a sense of humour who was proud of her sex appeal' (Korengold 1971, 50). In an interview published in the *New York Times* on the same day, Greer elaborated on her status as 'supergroupie' a subject on which she had first written in 1969 (1986b, 6–11). But she was no mere hanger-on. 'Supergroupies don't have to hang around hotel corridors', she told the *New York Times*. 'When you are one, as I have been, you get invited backstage. I think groupies are important because they demystify sex; they accept it as physical, and they aren't possessive about their conquests' (Greer 1971a; Weintraub 1971, 28).

Following Mailer, Greer would be both writer and subject of her proposed book ('in an essential way the book is about my sensibility'). On romantic fantasy, for example, she provided a 'reader, I married him' passage:

> The strength of the belief that a man should be stronger and older than his woman can hardly be exaggerated. I cannot claim to be fully emancipated from the dream that some enormous man, say six foot six, heavily shouldered and so forth to match, will crush me to his tweeds, look down into my eyes and leave the taste of heaven or the scorch of passion on my waiting lips. For three weeks I was married to him. (Greer 1971a)

On the nature of the vagina, Greer reported the unexpected benefits of diligent scholarship: 'I myself did not realize that the tissues of my vagina were quite normal until I saw a meticulously engraved dissection in an eighteenth-century anatomy textbook' (1971a, 39). And on make-up: 'The cheapest and some of the best fun are the colours used on stage in greasepaint. Kohl is the best eye make-up and the cheapest and can be bought in various forms' (Greer 1971a, 325).

One of the reasons for the book's appeal was its combination of subjective reportage and universalist argument: her analysis claimed to rest on personal experience yet be relevant to all women everywhere. Her draft synopsis described the ground she would cover:

> A piece on the female orgasm and female genitality in general. Then an examination of the moral stature of the female in Western culture, from virgin worship and misogyny to womanhood as sacred maytrdom. Then the reification of the female, the woman as thing, indicative of her owner's wealth, prestige, good taste, in the never ending competition with his male friends and colleagues. This ought to expand into a discussion of women in western literature ... [20]

As planning for *The Female Eunuch* became more detailed, it began to take its final shape. 'The book is written in short sections', she explained in the draft 'Summary', 'as unacademically as I knew how'. By now the book was directed to a more sympathetically imagined busy woman reader, 'a woman whose concentration is disturbed by other calls on her attention'. Hopefully she might experience a shock of recognition. 'Basically the book is aimed to direct her attention more critically to the forms of conditioning and exploitation in her every day environment.'[21] In providing the everyday woman with a language to describe the processes which oppressed her—'conditioning', 'stereotypes', 'sex objects', 'sex roles'—*The Female Eunuch* was influential in popularising a vocabulary that would inform popular feminist discourse over the next several decades.

The completed book was divided into five sections—Body, Soul, Love, Hate and Revolution—with 29 short sub-sections, some just a couple of pages in length, culminating in 'Revolution'. Women readers pressed for time could dip into the book at will, but if they read through to the endnotes, they would find a dazzling array of sources, many of them literary. For as soon as Greer was awarded a contract, she had to embark on a massive research program ordered on a series of index cards, now held in the Greer archive. She summoned evidence from a wide range of literary texts—Shakespeare, Milton, Plath, Ibsen, Blake, Hellman—as well as philosophical and theoretical writers such as Nietzche, Malinowski and Engels—popular sources, including contemporary women's and men's magazines and scientific studies from psychology, biology, and sociology.

Early in the introductory 'Summary', the reader encountered Cleaver: 'The Ultra-feminine must refuse any longer to countenance the Omnipotent Administrator' (Greer 1971a, 18). But not until the beginning of the second section of the book—significantly called 'Soul'—are we introduced to the 'Omnipotent Administrator' as the key figure in Eldridge Cleaver's 'Allegory of the Black Eunuchs' and we are returned to the original conception of the book (Greer 1971a, 59). If Cleaver could write a book about the 'soul of the Negro'—*Soul on Ice*—so Greer could explain the damaged soul of the castrated woman, the female eunuch.

One reason for *The Female Eunuch*'s astonishing success was its transnational reach. Unlike women's liberation texts that followed in Australia, for example, Anne Summers' *Damned Whores and God's Police* (1975) and *The Real Matilda* (1976) by Miriam Dixson and English accounts of women's oppression such as those by Rowbotham, Anna Davin, and Sally Alexander—*The Female Eunuch* eschewed historical explanations and specificities. Women's oppression was not the result of the particularities of a national past, the impact of the convict legacy, for example; their common castrated condition spanned time and place. Greer's metropolitan, indeed imperial location and perspective—based in London, the heart of empire—and her training in canonical sixteenth- and seventeenth-century English literature—augmented her confidence in making universalist claims and her authority as a writer.

'One is not born, but rather becomes a woman'

For all Greer's dismissal of earlier feminist writers and her bluestocking forebears in the draft proposals, her arguments actually bore a striking similarity to those enunciated by Mary Wollstonecraft in the late eighteenth-century and Simone de Beauvoir in the mid-twentieth century. 'The eternal feminine', de Beauvoir had written, corresponds to 'the black soul' (1987, 23). Here too the analogy worked to effect a disavowal of racial difference among women (Spelman 1991, 199–216).

Greer quoted Wollstonecraft on the same page as she introduced Cleaver's 'Black Eunuchs'. For all her claims to novelty, Greer's text can be located in a long tradition of feminist protest at women's supineness and self-deception. Greer, like Wollstonecraft and de Beauvoir was propelled into print by anger and frustration at women's apparent docility, their annoying femininity, their 'bad faith'. 'Whence comes this submission in the case of women?' de Beauvoir had asked in exasperation (1987, 18). Or as Greer observed: 'The cage door had opened but the canary had refused to fly out.' Directly echoing de Beauvoir on 'the metaphysical risk of a liberty in which ends and aims must be contrived without assistance', she insisted that 'Liberty is terrifying, but it is also liberating' (Greer 1971a, 19; de Beauvoir 1987, 21).

'One is not born, but rather becomes a woman', de Beauvoir declared at the opening of the chapter on Childhood in *The Second Sex* (1987, 295). Greer similarly announced that she would investigate 'how she comes to be made'. For all its declared sensationalism, *The Female Eunuch* was in many ways a deeply conventional feminist text. 'In order to understand how a female is castrated and becomes feminine', she explained, 'we must consider the pressures to which she is subjected from the cradle'. In 'The Formative Years' de Beauvoir had written of these pressures in chapters on 'Childhood', 'The

Young Girl' and 'Sexual Initiation'. Greer's chapters are called 'Baby', 'Girl', 'Puberty' and 'The Psychological Sell'.

In her proposals to the publisher, Greer had declared repeatedly that she did not like women. Wollstonecraft and de Beauvoir had similarly expressed their impatience at women's trivial lives and wily ways. Wollstonecraft despaired at women's timidity and unreason. 'All their thoughts', she complained,

> turn on things calculated to excite emotion and feeling, when they should reason, their conduct is unstable, and their opinions are wavering ... Fragile in every sense of the word, they are obliged to look up to man for every comfort. In the most trifling danger they cling to their support, with parasitical tenacity, piteously demanding succour ... In the name of reason, and even common sense, what can save such beings from contempt; even though they be soft and fair. (Wollstonecraft 1992, 152–153)

In her draft proposals, Greer had expressed her fear that she shared the 'contempt' men felt for women in explicit expressions of misogyny that would be deleted from the final text. By late 1970 'sisterhood' demanded nothing less.

Germaine Greer's archive is interesting and illuminating and she is to be commended for making it available to us in all its candour. On the one hand, it allows us to see how conventional in some ways were the impulses that drove her book—above all her frustration with women—and the forces that propelled her to write. On the other hand, the papers also register a sharp cultural break, a new departure. It was not women's lack of rational thought that enraged her, but their sexlessness. There was a new emphasis on the importance of sexual energy, virility and the desirability of heterosexual orgasm that owed much to Greer's libertarian background in Sydney, but it also derived from an infatuation with contemporary American writers, such as Cleaver, Hoffman and Mailer. And by the late 1960s, there was the imperative to grab media attention that owed much to the tactics of Yippies such as Hoffman and Rubin.

'TV time', Jerry Rubin had written, 'goes to those with the most guts and imagination'. Greer had plenty of both. She was 'the ballsy author of "the female eunuch"' (1972, 61) Her initial promise 'I shall suggest some very exciting but utterly unacceptable experimental measures for releasing female identity, a form of ["cunt" deleted and replaced by "Venus" power] ... ' appealed to the media in its simultaneous endorsement and refusal of phallocentrism. The subsequent confusions on the part of the male media and Greer's own testy second thoughts are evident in *Playboy's* long interview, when she repeatedly snapped at Nat Lehrman in response to his presumptions (1972).

Greer's simultaneous engagement with hundreds of thousands of women readers—an engagement facilitated and encouraged by the media attention—proved transformative as 'the feminist that even men like' became the writer who spoke to women about their lives in ways that ensured *The Female Eunuch* became 'the feminist bestseller of [a] generation', in Desley Deacon's words. Deacon still remembered 'the intense excitement' she felt when she read the book in 1971 (1999). Greer's papers contain many similar heartfelt responses. 'I have just finished reading The Female Eunuch', wrote American Dina Adler, in September, 1971, 'and, like thousands of other women throughout the country, I am sure, feel I owe you a debt of gratitude for expressing succinctly and wittily what we have felt inside for a long time'.[22] The Greer archive contains hundreds of such letters from women that will no doubt form the basis of many research projects to come. It was in these exchanges—in the conversations between a writer and hundreds of thousands of readers—that *The Female Eunuch* became the feminist book that changed women's lives.

Acknowledgment

My thanks to Lee-Ann Monk for her outstanding research assistance.

Notes

1. University of Melbourne Archives, Germaine Greer Archive, *The Female Eunuch* 'Editorial', 'Call It: The Most Difficult Part is the Synopsis', three pages typed, two pages handwritten, Box 216, 2014.0038.
2. Greer, Draft 'Summary', Greer Archive, Box 216.
3. Greer, Draft 'Summary', Greer Archive, Box 216.
4. Greer 'Editorial' [handwritten], 21 April 1969. Greer Archive, Box 216; the phenomenon of the 'Uncle Tom' in American Black culture was discussed extensively by Cleaver in *Soul on Ice* (1968).
5. Greer, 'Call It: The Most Difficult Part is the Synopsis', 'Synopsis', Greer Archive, Box 216.
6. Greer, 'Call It: The Most Difficult Part is the Synopsis', Greer Archive, Box 216.
7. Greer, *The Female Eunuch* Editorial, Greer Archive, Box 216.
8. Greer 'Summary', 2, Greer Archive, Box 216.
9. Greer, Draft 'Summary', 2, Greer Archive, Box 216.
10. Greer, 'Call It: The Most Difficult Part is the Synopsis', Greer Archive, Box 216.
11. Greer, Draft 'Summary', 11, Greer Archive, Box 216.
12. The 'problem of female identity' in Greer, Draft Synopsis, Greer Archive, Box 216.
13. Greer, 'Call It: The Most Difficult Part is the Synopsis', handwritten additional pages, Greer Archive, Box 216.
14. Greer, 'Call It: The Most Difficult Part is the Synopsis', handwritten additional pages, Greer Archive, Box 216.
15. Greer, 'Call It: The Most Difficult Part is the Synopsis', handwritten additional pages, Greer Archive, Box 216.
16. Greer, 'TFE Editorial', two pages handwritten, 21 April 1969, Greer Archive, Box 216.
17. Greer 'Call It: The Most Difficult Part is the Synopsis', extra pages handwritten, Greer Archive, Box 216.
18. Greer 'Call It: The Most Difficult Part is the Synopsis' typed pages, Greer Archive, Box 216.
19. Greer 'Synopsis', Geer Archive, Box 216 (Alomes 1999, 234). Alomes cites his source as 'personal communication from Sonny Mehta', which suggests that Mehta retained copies of the original proposal given to him by Greer, as this is also her exact wording.
20. Greer, 'Call It: The Most Difficult Part is the Synopsis', Greer Archive, Box 216.
21. Greer, Draft 'Summary', 3–4, Greer Archive, Box 216.
22. Dina Adler to Germaine Greer, 24 September 1971, Greer papers, Box 218.

Funding

This work was supported by ARC Discovery [grant number DP 110103669].

References

Adelaide, Debra. 1998. "It Changed my Life". *Weekend Australian*, May 2–3, 12.
Albert, Judith Clavir, and Stewart Edward Albert, eds. 1984. *The Sixties Papers: Documents of a Rebellious Decade*, 443. New York: Praeger Publishers.
Alderson, Maggie. 2012. "The Books that Changed Me". *Sun-Herald*, January 1.
Alomes, Stephen. 1999. *When London Calls: The Expatriation of Australian Creative Artists to Britain*. Melbourne: Cambridge University Press.
de Beauvoir, Simone. 1987. *The Second Sex*. Harmondsworth: Penguin.
Bell, Lynne. 1969. "Interview with Germaine Greer." *Sydney Morning Herald*, July 31.
Bongiorno, Frank. 2013. "Sensational Sexualities: Germaine Greer's *The Female Eunuch* and Dennis Altman's *Homosexual: Oppression and Liberation*." In *Telling Stories: Australian Life and Literature 1935–2012*, edited by Tanya Dalziell and Paul Genoni, 294–300. Melbourne: Monash University.
Britain, Ian. 1997. *Once an Australian: Journeys with Barry Humphries, Clive James, Germaine Greer and Robert Hughes*. Melbourne: Oxford University Press.
Bulbeck, Chilla. 1997. *Living Feminism: The Impact of the Women's Movement on Three Generations of Australian Women*. Melbourne: Cambridge University Press.
Cleaver, Eldridge. 1968. *Soul on Ice*. New York: McGraw-Hill.
Connolly, Ray. 1970. "The Strange and Eccentric Worlds of Dr Greer." *Herald*, January 14, 21.
Coote, Anna, and B. Campbell. 1987. *Sweet Freedom: The Struggle for Women's Liberation*. Oxford: Blackwell.
Deacon, Desley. 1999. "Tilting at windmills." *Women's Review of Books* XVI: 8–16.
Dreifus, Claudia. 1971. "The Selling of a Feminist." *The Nation*, June 7.
Dunstan, Keith. 2004. "Germaine Greer." In *The Best Australian Profiles*, edited by Matthew Ricketson, 52–64. Melbourne: Black.
Friedan, Betty. 1965. *The Feminine Mystique* (New York: Norton, 1963). Harmondsworth: Penguin.
Geismar, Maxwell. 1968. 'Introduction' to Eldridge Cleaver *Soul on Ice*. New York: McGraw-Hill.
Greer, Germaine. 1971a. *The Female Eunuch*. London: MacGibbon and Kee.
Greer, Germaine. 1971b. 'My Mailer Problem' *Esquire* September, reprinted in Greer, Germaine 1986. *The Madwoman's Underclothes: Essays and Occasional Writings 1968–85*. London: Picador.
Greer, Germaine. 1972. "Interview." *Playboy*, January.
Greer, Germaine. 1984. "Interview." In *No Return Ticket*, edited by Clyde Packer 85–99. Pymble: Angus and Robertson.
Greer, Germaine. 1986a. 'The Slag-Heap Erupts' Reprinted in Germaine Greer, *The Madwoman's Underclothes: Essays and Occasional Writings 1968–85*. London: Picador.
Greer, Germaine. 1986b. 'A Groupie's Vision' Reprinted in Greer, *The Madwoman's Underclothes: Essays and Occasional Writings 1968–85*. London: Picador. 6–11.
Greer, Germaine. 1986c. 'My Mailer Problem' Reprinted in Greer, The Madwoman's Underclothes: Essays and Occasional Writings 1968–85. London: Picador.
Grenville, Kate. 2009. "The Books that Changed Me." *Sun-Herald*, August 30.
Hoffman, Abbie. 2000. *The Autobiography of Abbie Hoffman*. San Francisco, CA: First Four Walls Eight Windows Edition. First Published Putnam, 1980.
Jezer, Marty. 1992. *Abbie Hoffman: American Rebel*. New Brunswick, NJ: Rutgers University Press.
King, Nene. 1971. "Earthquake Greer." *Sydney Morning Herald*, May 13.
Korengold, Robert. 1971. "Interview with Germaine Greer." *Newsweek*, March 22, 50.
Lake, Marilyn, and H. Reynolds. 2008. *Drawing the Global Colour Line: White Men's Countries and the International Challenge of Racial Equality*. Cambridge: Cambridge University Press.

Life Magazine Cover. 1971. *Saucy Feminist that Even Men Like*, May 7.

Lilburn, Sandra, Susan Magarey, and Susan Sheridan. 2000. "Celebrity Feminism as Synthesis: Germaine Greer, the Female Eunuch and the Australian Print Media." *Continuum: Journal of Media and Cultural Studies* 14: 335–348.

Mailer, Norman. 1957. "The White Negro." *Dissent Magazine*, Fall. https://www.dissentmagazine.org/online_articles/the-white-negro.

Mailer, Norman. 1971. *The Prisoner of Sex*. London: Weidenfeld and Nicolson. First Published in *Harper's* March 1971.

McGrath, Ann. 1999. "The Female Eunuch in the Suburbs: Reflections on Adolescence, Autobiography and History-Writing." *Journal of Popular Culture* 33: 177–190.

Mitchell, Juliet. 1966. "Women: The Longest Revolution." *New Left Review* 1/40: 11–37.

Morgan, Robyn. 1970. *Sisterhood if Powerful: An Anthology of Writings from the Women's Liberation Movement*. New York: Vintage.

Raskin, Jonah. 1996. *For the Hell of It: The Life and Times of Abbie Hoffman*, 174. Berkley: University of California Press.

Reed, Evelyn. 1971. "Feminism and 'The Female Eunuch'." *International Socialist Review*, July–August.

Rowbotham, Sheila. 1970. *The Book That Men Love and Women Hate*. London: Oz, London, November–December.

Rowbotham, Sheila. 1990. "The Beginnings of Women's Liberation in Britain." In *Once a Feminist: Stories of a Generation*, edited by Michelene Wandor, 28–42. London: Virago, London.

Roxon, Lilian. 1971. "A Literary Bombshell." *Sydney Morning Herald*, April 10.

Segal, Lynne. 1987. *Is the Future Female? Troubled Thoughts on Contemporary Feminism*. London: Virago.

Spelman, Elizabeth V. 1991. "Simone de Beauvoir and Women: Just Who Does She Think "We" Is?" In *Feminist Interpretations and Political Theory*, edited by Mary Lyndon Shanley, Mary Lyndon, and Carol Pateman, 119–216. Cambridge: Polity Press.

Spongberg, Mary. 1993. "If She's So Great, How Come So Many Pigs Dig Her?" *Women's History Review* 2: 407–419.

Tanner, Leslie B. 1971. *Voices from Women's Liberation*. New York: Mentor.

Wallace, Michele. 1979. *Black Macho and the Myth of the Superwoman*. London: John Calder.

Wallace, Christine. 1997. *Greer: Untamed Shrew*. Sydney: Macmillan.

Wandor, Michelene. 1990. *Once a Feminist: Stories of a Generation*. London: Virago.

Weintraub, Judith. 1971. "Interview with Germaine Greer." *New York Times*, March 22.

Wollstonecraft, Mary. 1992. *A Vindication of the Rights of Women*. London: Penguin.

Zito, Tom. 1971. "The Greer Career." *Washington Post*, April 22.

The record keeper

Rachel Buchanan

ABSTRACT
Germaine Greer is an exceptional record keeper. Since the 1950s, Greer has retained and protected papers relating to her extraordinary public and private lives and her diligence has resulted in the Germaine Greer Archive, a large, world-class collection now held by the University of Melbourne Archives. As curator of the archive, I am now the record keeper. This article explains two connections—one personal and the other institutional—that are shaping the way I think about Greer's papers.

Germaine Greer began keeping things as an undergraduate student at the University of Melbourne in the late 1950s. At first it was mostly books, notebooks, essays and lecture notes connected with academic research and teaching but by the late 1960s the keeping expanded to newspaper clippings and shopping lists, hotel receipts and party invitations, proofs, postcards, wine labels, flyers and a funny little orange British School of Motoring appointment book connected with fraught attempts at learning to drive in 1972. After *The Female Eunuch* was published, letters became an especially pressing category of thing. Greer has kept thousands that she received, along with carbon copies of her replies. In the early 1970s, her responses to readers were often long and peppered with jokes, advice and rueful personal anecdotes. But Greer's keeping did not stop with paper. It eventually encompassed other things: cassette and video tapes, some photos and vinyl records, digital audio recordings, hard drives, discs, a reel of 16 mm film.

Greer left Australia for Cambridge in 1964 and for the next 20 years she moved often. She lived in Cambridge, London, Leamington Spa, Tuscany and Tulsa, Oklahoma. She travelled to India, Bangladesh, Cuba, New Zealand, India, Vietnam, Ethiopia, Brazil and elsewhere and had many trips back to Australia. In the past decade, Greer has spent extended periods in southern Queensland. In 2001 she bought Cave Creek, a 65-hectare rainforest there, and set up a rehabilitation scheme for it (Greer 2013).[1] Somehow, Greer's papers and other things were not lost, destroyed, damaged or dispersed in all these moves. She considered her hoard worth protecting and did so. The effort must have been considerable. The survival of the collection is proof of how much Greer valued the evidence of her own life and the evidence her things contained about the lives of others, not just famous people but hundreds of ordinary ones as well (McKemmish 1996; Piggott 2007, 237–258). The scope of the collection is evidence of the power of feminism as a social movement and the charisma of Greer as one of its idiosyncratic exponents.

After 40 years of keeping, Greer created several detailed inventories of her papers. A catalogue prepared by Greer is a 230-page record of the arrangement of the material by year. Each year is separated into drawers that describe the nature of the work or correspondence. For instance, 1969 contains work filed in drawers marked author, journalism, television, academic and correspondence. Another 87-page inventory, prepared by an assistant, lists Greer's film, television and radio appearances from 1963 to 2014.

The things had become an entity. They assumed a title—an upper-case noun—and, like most notable literary archives, a market value. In 2013, the University of Melbourne bought the Germaine Greer archive and in mid-2014, the University Archivist, Dr Katrina Dean, went to Professor Greer's house in Essex, England, to pack the collection up. This task took three weeks. The enormous collection was housed in 150 drawers in dozens of black or wood veneer filing cabinets in either Greer's office or on the first floor of an outbuilding described as 'the hutch'. Once packed, the material was shipped to the University of Melbourne Archives (UMA). The 476 boxes occupy five decks of floor to ceiling shelves in a bay in the store. The correspondence series takes up 120 square boxes, 11 squat boxes hold Greer's index cards, several long flat boxes contain photographs and other small ones contain microfilm and a hard drive. What was a domestic collection is now an institutional one.

My connection with these things began in October 2015 when I was appointed curator, Germaine Greer Archive. It is interesting to have the name Germaine Greer in my job title. It is a fact that has not yet been met with indifference. People are eager to tell me what they think of Greer. Sometimes they ask for my opinion as well. I usually say I do not have one. My job is to care for and understand a collection of records. Several quotations have been helpful with this work. One is something I read while I was access examining box 16, which is from the 'C' section of the voluminous correspondence series. The item is in the Carmen Callil folder. Callil, who is also from Melbourne, was the founder of Virago Press. One letter concerns Callil's sketch of Greer, written in 1987, for *The Sunday Times* in London. The newspaper was celebrating its 25th anniversary with a feature on the 25 most important people of the past 25 years.

'I rang you to talk to you about it because I didn't want to write anything you would hate', Callil explains in her letter to Greer.[2] Callil was worried that her brief piece did not convey how 'wonderfully amusing and ebullient you are'. The unedited version of the piece was attached. In it, Callil describes *The Female Eunuch* as 'a brilliant polemic' that 'took women by the scruff of the neck and shook them into taking charge of their own lives'.

'There is no measure by which to gauge how the world was changed because of her', Callil wrote of Greer and *The Female Eunuch*. 'A poll among women would certainly show that she influenced them more than any other writer of her time. Simone de Beauvoir's influence was intellectual, Betty Friedan's practical. Germaine went beyond both: her courage was contagious and she gave women heart.'

'In return she has been misunderstood and misread, contributing to this by her ebullient sense of humour and her pleasure in going too far', Callil said. This last phrase—the pleasure in going too far—has stuck. These records are evidence of the life of someone who enjoys being provocative and seeks, via her actions and words, to 'stimulate thought'. (Greer 1986, 1)[3]

As well as reading through the records and cataloguing them, I am reading my way through Greer's published books and essays, beginning with the ones held in University of Melbourne libraries. I enjoy art books and was pleased to see Greer had contributed an essay to a handsome one on British artist and filmmaker Tacita Dean (Royoux et al. 2006). The two women are friends. I read Greer's piece then flicked through the rest. Marina Warner's interview with Dean fascinated me. The second helpful quote was here. Dean says:

> The idea of chance has always interested me, but I think it depends as much on a facility to notice—being in a state of grace—as anything else, so that you are open to it. When you are actually immersed in something you do notice—well I do—the connections. (Royoux et al. 2006, 13)

That is what I am seeking in my work with the Greer Archive: an open-minded engagement, an immersion, an ability to see connections. Connections help create context. The meaning of a document in an archive comes from its relationships to other records in that archive and to the people or organisations who created it. In the case of personal recordkeeping, especially a collection as large as Greer's, the motivations of the creator are also worth considering (Bettington et al. 2008, 18).

Two different relationships are shaping the way I am thinking about the Greer Archive. One is personal, the other institutional.

Although the archive is now separated from its creator, Greer's body is somehow imprinted on the records. There are the physical impressions created by her pen—the lovely handwriting, the sketches, doodles and notes—her typewriter and her keyboard. There are the records of her voice in the audio diaries and speeches as well, but this relationship between the creator's body and the records is more pervasive than mere touch. Greer's body has been the primary source for her most influential books. It is her first archive. What does it mean to be in a woman's body? What does a woman's body do? How does it work? How is it different from a man's? What does it mean to bleed each month? What does it mean to stop bleeding? Or have children? These are some of the big questions that Greer is asking of her body and answering in her work.

Her young woman's body, its energy, its vigour, its sexiness and its power, was the fuel for *The Female Eunuch* (1970). Her middle-aged body powered *Sex and Destiny* (1986), *Daddy, We Hardly Knew You* (1989) and *The Change: Women Aging, and the Menopause* (1991) and *The Whole Woman* (1999), her ageing body, slower, wiser, more determined, is behind *White Beech* (2013). The determination to find a scientific understanding for growth and difference remains just as intense but the focus has shifted from biology to botany, from people to trees.

Greer began to research the manuscript that would become *The Female Eunuch* in 1969, the year she turned 30. Body, the first section of the book, contains six chapters: Gender; Bones; Curves; Hair; Sex and The Wicked Womb. Together, these chapters were an exploration of 'the sex of cells' and what 'chromosomal difference' between women and men might mean (Greer 1971,14). *Sex and Destiny: The Politics of Human Fertility* (1984) came out when Greer was 45 and nearing the end of her own fertility. It contains the startling assertion that women in the West are having fewer children not 'because we are concerned about the population explosion or because we feel we cannot afford children, but because we do not like children' (Greer 1986, 2). The book is dedicated to two of her godchildren. She did not have a child of her own. *The Change* was published when Greer was 53. There is no need to labour the point but Greer's insistence on linking her research with the body explains the rawness of some of the material in this archive, not just Greer's private correspondence but her readers' stories of love affairs, abortions, rape, menopause, childbirth and motherhood.

It is easy to get caught up in the exceptional nature of this archive, its depth and diversity, the wild humour and energy of so many of the documents but what happens if the Greer Archive is considered in relationship to the many other relevant collections it shares shelf space with? UMA has one of Australia's most significant collections of records relating to the women's liberation movement and the feminisms that have flourished since then as well as the early movements that fed into women's lib. Via individual donations, such as the papers of peace activists Dorothy and Ralph Gibson and through individual photographs in the archives of the Communist Party of Australia, we have many records relating to 1960s women's anti-war activism, especially the Save Our Sons anti-conscription movement.[4] What might be gained by reading Communist Party photographs of a handful of Save Our Sons protesters at the Marrickville Army Barracks in New South Wales in the late 1960s next to celebrity photographer Harry Benson's photographs of Germaine Greer marching in the enormous Vietnam War Out Now Rally in Washington in April 1971? What could this show us about how local movements work alongside or against global ones?

UMA's feminist archives are especially valuable because the archive began collecting material relating to the second wave of feminism in Australia as it occurred (Dean 2013, 2).[5] Papers about the Women's Electoral Lobby (WEL) and its 1972 federal election campaign were donated to UMA in 1974 via the lobby's University of Melbourne graduates and associates. One striking poster is a close up black and white image of a young woman's face. Viewers are advised to: *Think W.E.L Before You Vote. Equal education, work and pay opportunities—free contraception—child care—welfare benefits.*[6]

The Greer Archive is also surrounded by the truly epic Victorian Women's Liberation and Lesbian Feminist Archives (VWLLFA for short!). The archive is cared for by a collective that began with a women's liberation reading group in 1982. Members realised that women's liberation publications and ephemera were already 'hard to come by or had been destroyed' and so the archive was born.[7] The VWLLFA contains 150 individual collections and it is still being added to. Lesbian festivals, abortion action campaigns, women's studies centres, women against rape, halfway houses, community theatre, Aboriginal reconciliation study groups, feminist book fairs and the papers of dozens of Melbourne women involved in feminist activities are some of the holdings. Posters, banners and T-shirts, sport slogans with the same vital, direct energy as Greer's feminist writing: Fuck Housework; Kids Have Rights; Don't be too polite girls!; The best man for a job is a woman; If it's not appropriate for women it's not appropriate; Maybe he's raping you and Dyke Lightning. They are evidence of a local movement every bit as passionate, provocative, wickedly funny and urgent as the best of Greer's writing.

Feminist publisher Susan Hawthorn (Spinifex) and McPhee Gribble's feminist offshoot Sisters also have their papers here as does Sugar and Snails Press Co-operative (1974–1999), a Box Hill collective that published non-sexist children's books. Greer's archive contains ephemera relating to both American and British women's publishing collectives and provides an international counterpoint to all the work happening here in Australia. UMA also has the archive of the University of Melbourne's George Paton Gallery. Under the directorship of Kiffy Rubbo, the gallery exhibited feminist, Marxist, Buddhist, performance art, experimental art and video art, including the work of Dianne Arbus (who photographed Greer in New York in 1971).[8]

A recent acquisition is the papers of Renate Klein, beginning with the 1980s and Klein's involvement with the emerging discipline of women's studies in Europe, the USA and then Australia. Klein's papers document early feminist responses to reproductive technologies, including the work of a group called the Feminist International Network of Resistance to Reproductive and Genetic Engineering and the international debates among feminists about emergent In vitro fertilisation procedures.[9] From the research notes for *Sex and Destiny* and *The Whole Woman* to research notes for an unrealised 1978 television series called *The Story of Human Reproduction*, the contents of the Greer Archive have many overlaps with the Klein one and aid understanding of a strand of women's political activism that has almost completely disappeared from public discourse. Greer has truly joined the women's movement by sending her archive here.

Notes

1. See Cave Creek Rehabilitation Scheme, http://gondwanarainforest.org/cave-creek, accessed 25 February 2016.
2. UMA, Germaine Greer Archive, 2014.0038; Box 216; Carmen Callil folder, typescript, 'Germaine Greer: For the *Sunday Times* Colour Magazine' attached to letter, Callil to Greer, 23 January 1987.
3. The full quote is: 'Some books are incitements to action, none of them good books, for the principal function of writing, even polemical writing, is to stimulate thought.'
4. UMA, Papers of Dorothy and Ralph Gibson, 1981.0153 and 1983.0085; UMA, A Save Our Sons demonstration at Marrickville Army Barracks, New South Wales, 1991.0152.0014 and UMA, Germaine Greer Archive, 2014.0038, LIFE Photograph Album.
5. Dean notes: 'The women's movement was an early contributor to UMA's collections, and in sufficient quantities for the Archives Board of Management to consider seeking from the National Council of Women a grant to catalogue these holdings.'
6. UMA, WEL Poster Think W.E.L. Before You Vote, 2015.0037
7. I want to thank deputy archivist Sue Fairbanks for her assistance with understanding UMA's extensive feminist archives, including the VWLLFA; the Sisters Publishing Archive, 1999.0016; the Sugar & Snails Press Co-operative, 1991.0132 and papers of Susan Hawthorne 2014.0033.
8. With thanks to assistant archivist Georgie Ward for drawing my attention to this archive. The University of Melbourne George Paton Gallery Collection, 1990.0144; Vivian (2008); Also 'Creativity & Correspondence: The George Paton Gallery Archive' http://blogs.unimelb.edu.au/archives/selected-images-from-recent-exhibition-creativity-correspondence-the-george-paton-gallery-archive-1971-1990-and-other-images-from-the-archive/ (accessed 22 December 2015).
9. UMA, Papers of Renate Klein, 2014.0034.

References

Bettington, Jackie, Kim Eberhard, Rowena Loo, and Clive Smith, eds. 2008. *Keeping Archives*. 3rd ed. Canberra: Australian Society of Archivists.

Dean, Katrina. 2013. "Collecting the Archives of Protest." *Protest!* Newspaper produced to accompany exhibition, University of Melbourne Archives.

Greer, Germaine. (1970) 1971. *The Female Eunuch*. New ed. London: Paladin.

Greer, Germaine. 1986. *Sex and Destiny: The Politics of Human Fertility*. New York: Harper & Row.

Greer, Germaine. 1999. *The Whole Woman*. London: Doubleday.

Greer, Germaine. 2013. *White Beech: The Rainforest Years*. London: Bloomsbury.

McKemmish, Sue. 1996. "Evidence of Me." *Archives and Manuscripts* 45 (3): 174–187.

Piggott, Michael. 2007. "Human Behaviour and the Making of Records and Archives." *Archives and Social Sciences: A Journal of Interdisciplinary Research* 1: 237–258.

Royoux, Jean-Christophe, Tacita Dean, Marina Warner, and Germaine Greer. 2006. *Tacita Dean*. London: Phaidon Press.

Vivian, Helen. ed. 2008. *When You Think About Art: The Ewing & George Paton Galleries 1971-2008*, Melbourne: Macmillan.

Resurrecting Germaine's theory of cuntpower

Megan Le Masurier

ABSTRACT
In the early years of the second wave, two very different approaches to female sexuality and feminist politics were in circulation, Anne Koedt's 'The Myth of the Vaginal Orgasm' and Germaine Greer's theory of cuntpower. While the clitoral orgasm became the 'feminist orgasm' during these years, Greer's more open and genitally inclusive theory of cuntpower encouraged women to explore the variations of their own heterosexuality in the name of women's and sexual liberation. This article will argue that Greer's ideas about cuntpower are worth resurrecting and integrating into our understanding of second wave feminist sexual politics. It will also argue that Greer's utilisation of the media allowed her ideas to influence ordinary women's understanding of the potential of their sexuality, their right to orgasm and its connection to women's liberation.

In the early years of the second wave, the orgasm became a battleground between different visions of feminist sexual politics, played out on the intimate field of women's bodies. The received wisdom about the 1970s is that in terms of both feminist and popular understandings of female sexual pleasure, the clitoris dominated the decade. Within dominant strands of second wave sexual politics, the clitoral orgasm became the feminist orgasm—an embodied site of a particular commitment to feminism. Anne Koedt's pamphlet, 'The Myth of the Vaginal Orgasm', written in 1968 and widely circulated in the following years, was a core text behind this position. The vaginal orgasm was ridiculed as a delusion, an internalisation of male definitions of female sexuality. As the political intensity built around the 'feminist orgasm', women who experienced orgasms in other ways and women who enjoyed penetration, were often bullied into silence, including feminist-identifying women. Germaine Greer, however, would not be silenced. In her journalism of the late 1960s and early 1970s for the underground press, and in *The Female Eunuch*, Greer insisted upon the importance of an active female heterosexuality and what she termed cuntpower.[1] Cuntpower was a claim not just to the varieties of orgasm women could experience—vaginal, clitoral, or combined—and the pleasures of penetration, but to the ecstasy that could result, transforming women from their eunuch status and releasing the energy necessary for revolution.

In expounding the theory of cuntpower through her writings and media performances, Greer secured her isolation from many feminist activists, but also secured her popularity amongst ordinary heterosexual women struggling for a way to find sexual pleasure and equality in their everyday lives. Reviled by many in the second wave for what they saw as promoting the image of the feminist as 'a superfuck' (Coote and Campbell 1982, 240), and using the media for personal gain rather than that of the women's movement, Greer has rarely been taken seriously in the accounts of the sexuality debates of this time (see Spongberg 1993). This article will argue that Greer's ideas about cuntpower are worth exhuming and integrating into our understanding of second wave feminist sexual politics. It will also argue that Greer's utilisation of the media allowed her ideas to influence ordinary women's understanding of the potential of their sexuality, their right to orgasm and its connection to a kind of liberation. The term 'ordinary' is used to describe those women who did not identify as women's liberationists or as feminists, who did not share the privileges of class and education that characterised most of the women involved in the movement, and those who found radical feminism's critique of the family, the state, and men alienating.

Before these two divergent positions on feminist sexual politics—the clitoral orgasm and cuntpower—are explored in depth, it is important to reiterate the connection between sexual and women's liberation in the early years of the second wave and how this connection was severed, or at least sublimated, within official/political feminism in the 'sex wars'.

Women's liberation and sexual liberation

The beginnings of the second wave are often painted in the colours of disenchantment with the experience of the sexism of men involved with radical politics. Sexually, the role of women was famously positioned by Stokely Carmichael as 'prone' (Garton 2004, 223).[2] The sexual sweet talk was the words of liberation from capitalist repression of sexuality and the 'hang-ups' of bourgeois morality. As many of the women involved in radical politics in the 1960s have noted, more sex with more partners did not mean more liberation. The *Playboy* ethic for revolutionaries drove many women to recognise sexism as an oppression as great, if not greater, than imperialism and class, and to form the early groups of Women's Liberation (Curthoys 1992; Lake 1999; Segal 1994). Listening to the memories of many feminists involved in the early years of Women's Liberation, however, there is another story told about the role of sexual liberation. While sexuality may have been the source of women's oppression, for many it promised to be the source of their liberation. 'Feminists in the late 1960s joined sexual liberation to women's liberation, claiming that one without the other would keep women second-class citizens' (Gerhard 2000, 465). In a frank exchange in the early eighties, US feminist Deirdre English spoke of the mythologising that was already occurring about the 'sexual revolution':

> It's very popular now to say that the sexual revolution of the sixties was incredibly oppressive to women ... The sexism was there, but ... the raised sexual expectations created enormous social and sexual gains for women ... Many women were actually able to change the way that men made love with them as well as the way they made love with men ... Women were fighting for sexual rights and often getting them. (English, Hollibaugh, and Rubin 1982, 42)

For many women, the experience of sexual freedom was intoxicating. It gave them a taste of sexual pleasure, independence, and possibility. Jane Gallop writes of her early experience of feminism as a 'double transformation':

> The disaffected, romantic, passive young woman I had been gained access simultaneously to real learning and to an active sexuality. One achievement cannot be separated from the other ... feminism made me feel sexy and smart; feminism felt smart and sexy. (1997, 5–6)

Ann Snitow recalled how she had felt sexually oppressed and depressed before feminism opened her body to the empowering possibilities of active desire: '... before the movement I found sexual power unthinkable. Now angry and awake, I felt for the first time what the active eroticism of men might be like' (1989, 219). Lynne Segal notes that for all the confusion and uncertainty, these 'liberated' heterosexual experiences could be 'a delight in the affirmation of self' (1994, 9):

> The fight against sexual hypocrisy and for sexual openness and pleasure provided much of its [women's liberation's] early inspiration, as women decided that pleasure was as much a social and political as a personal matter. These issues were not only central to the genesis of feminism, they remain central to the majority of women's lives today. (xi–xii)

The ideas behind sexual liberation carried *into* the early years of women's liberation. The Australian feminist historian Jill Julius Matthews reflected:

> For a while in the early seventies, feminism was able to hold on to both positions: the end to be achieved by overcoming women's oppression was a human liberation in which true equality and freedom in sexuality as in all else would be enjoyed by all. (1997, xii)

In the 'sex wars' of the 1970s and 1980s this early entwining of sexual and women's liberation seemed to disappear. In trying to explore female sexuality outside structures of sexism or sexual practices designed, it was argued, to solely benefit male desires and pleasures, the practice of penetrative sex (and for some feminists the very institution of heterosexuality) came under serious question. Some feminists judged heterosexuality harshly, publicly denouncing it as anything from sleeping with the enemy to legalised prostitution, masochism, and/or patriarchal brainwashing (Albury 2002, 33–38). Feminists such as Carol Smart have described the intensity of this debate: 'It was as if there were really only two available positions; one which seemed to gloat over the mistakes of heterosexual women and one which seemed to apologise for being heterosexual' (1996, 168). Ellen Willis reflected:

> The emphasis had changed from confronting men with their petty tyrannies in the bedroom —the myriad small acts of selfishness, ignorance, and egotism that interfered with women's sexual pleasure—to denouncing rape as the paradigm for male dominance. In retrospect it is clear that we were witnessing a pivotal moment in the movement's history ... many feminists' utopian hopes gave way to apocalyptic despair. (1994, 46)

Focus on the dangers rather than the pleasures of heterosexuality came to dominate internal debates.[3] Male sexuality began to look like a 'continuum of violence' and straight feminists were left angry, resentful and for a time, silenced.

> Many heterosexual feminists had no intention of suppressing their desires for sexual encounters and relationships with men, but I think that many of us did feel undermined and confused, if not guilty, by the accusation that we were too 'male-identified' and 'soft on men'. (Segal 1994, 58)

Anna Coote and Beatrix Campbell explained how heterosexual feminists had been driven onto the defensive: 'They felt roughed up by the very movement in which they had sought safety' (1982, 243). This was the sex war to come. But there had been earlier disputes amongst women's liberationists about the nature of female sexuality and 'truth' of the female orgasm.

The feminist orgasm

Masters and Johnson's work in the sexual laboratory of the 1960s had revealed the clitoris as the centre of female sexual response. In their best-selling *Human Sexual Response* (1966), the authors had explained that women's most intense orgasms came not from intercourse but from masturbation. The radical implication of Masters and Johnson's work was that intercourse was not essential for female sexual pleasure. The Freudian orthodoxy of the clitoral orgasm as 'immature' and vaginal orgasm as the site of adjusted and mature female sexuality was turned on its head (45–68). Masters and Johnson's intention was not to suggest that women could dispense with men but to strengthen the marital couple via better and orgasmic sex for women.

Anne Koedt based much of her influential article 'The Myth of the Vaginal Orgasm' on the insights of Masters and Johnson but put them to quite a different use. The clitoris, the 'female equivalent of the penis', is the centre of sexual sensitivity. The vagina 'is not a highly sensitive area and is not constructed to achieve orgasm' ([1970] 1973, 198). Every orgasm, no matter how it felt, was clitoral (199). Because of the male need to have penetrative sex:

> women have been defined sexually in terms of what pleases men; our own biology has not been properly analysed. Instead, we are fed a myth of the liberated woman and her vaginal orgasm—an orgasm that in fact does not exist. (199)

Koedt's radical interpretation was to suggest that the clitoral orgasm threatened the 'heterosexual institution' (206). Men were potentially 'sexually expendable' when penis in vagina was not necessary for orgasmic female sex. 'It would indicate that sexual pleasure was obtainable from either men or women, thus making heterosexuality not an absolute but an option' (206).

Koedt gave an early version of this paper at the first national Women's Liberation Conference in the USA in 1968. Long and detailed conversations followed as women exchanged highly personal details about their orgasms, lack thereof, and their sexual fantasies. It was an example of the consciousness-raising that was to define the early years of women's liberation. But even here, in 1968, the vaginal orgasm was ridiculed and one woman felt compelled to apologise after her claim of having experienced a vaginal orgasm had been 'exposed' (Segal 1994, 25). Jane Gerhard argues that the clitoral orgasm became the marker of 'the feminist'.

> Feminists reclaimed the orgasm from experts and male lovers and reinfused it with new symbolic meanings. Within second-wave feminism, the female orgasm came to represent women's self-determination, making 'the great orgasm debate' central, not incidental, to the project of women's liberation. (2001, 82)

In Sydney, piles of Koedt's paper were stacked in Women's Liberation House. Versions circulated attributed to a different author (Lake 1999, 221) and the article was used as the basis for many consciousness-raising sessions (Bulbeck 1997, 36). The 'Orgasm Meeting' there was attended by scores of women talking about their own experiences. Liz Fell, a libertarian feminist at the time, recalled 'there were as many orgasms as there were women... There was no way of neatly classifying them. It was revelatory for many women there I think, that there was no right or wrong way' (quoted in Wallace [1997] 2000, 206). Anne Summers has described 'The Myth of the Vaginal Orgasm' as 'one of the most provocative early writings to come out of America... startling stuff. No one was yet speaking frankly about sex or sexual organs' (1999, 261). The Adelaide Women's Liberation Movement (WLM) re-published the article as a pamphlet in 1970 with an introduction by Summers who disputed some of Koedt's conclusions and recalls that the Adelaide WLM 'did not identify with the overall thesis' (261). 'Most women do experience desire for penetration', she wrote. And the 'thinly veiled lesbianism' was not a solution that would sexually satisfy all women (262).

Although the political impetus behind these discussions of women's orgasms was based in consciousness-raising techniques where women's experiences were privileged over male expertise, the democratic desire to hear—and accept—all women's experiences came to be over-ridden by the importance of the clitoral orgasm to feminist identity politics at the time. What had begun as an open discussion of varied orgasmic experiences turned into a regulative and normative theory where clitoral orgasm equalled feminist —and therefore vaginal orgasm or desire for penetration equalled non-feminist. As Alice Echols notes, the attempt to overcome old prescriptions would engender new ones and women who claimed to have vaginal orgasms were shamed into apologising (1989, 111–112). Many more were confused and silenced. The myth of the vaginal orgasm became an incontrovertible 'truth' in the feminist movement. 'Gale', writing in the Australian independent women's liberation periodical *Mejane* in 1971, for example, stated, 'This devastating myth ... has been the curse of women throughout the western world' (13). Annamarie Jagose notes that since the 1970s, 'a prominent strand of feminist discourse on orgasm has endorsed the sexological reversal ... that prioritizes the clitoris over the previously celebrated vagina' (2013, 25).

The new findings of 'scientia sexualis' were marshalled in the service of feminist politics. The new sexual normativity of the clitoral orgasm led to a stigmatisation, indeed a construction as mythical, of what became its necessary 'other', the vaginal orgasm, the deluded orgasm of 'false consciousness'. What a feminist did about penetrative sex with men (or even, for some theorists, with women) divided the movement during this period. Feminist anthropologist Muriel Dimen looked back at this time of sexual 'political correctness' in the second wave:

> The clitoral orgasm became public knowledge in 1969 because feminists made it so. But then the clitoral orgasm became the only politically correct orgasm to have, consequently foreshortening exploration and, at best, confusing, at worst, marginalizing, those who had a different experience. (1984, 146)

The focus on the feminist clitoral orgasm would prove to be both a revelation for many women and a strategic blunder for a feminism that wanted to represent, and speak for, all women. The heterosexual feminist who desired penetration was 'othered'—even, we could say, politically pathologised—by a dominant strand of activist/theoretical feminism. Germaine Greer, isolated from the women's movement for many reasons (see Spongberg 1993), epitomised this otherness in her writings about cuntpower.

Cuntpower

Cuntpower has its origins in Greer's experience as a libertarian in the late 1950s and 1960s and her experience of the counterculture in London. Greer had embraced the ideas and lifestyle of the libertarian Push until she left Sydney for England in 1964. The Push was a collection of 'critical drinkers' in the 1950 and 1960s, inspired by the libertarian ideas of John Anderson, an influential Professor of Philosophy at the University of Sydney. The group was anti-censorship and was opposed to sexual repression, which Anderson linked to conservative fears of social disruption. 'The group's equation of sexual repression with political authoritarianism was the basis of a dynamic in which free sex was the marker of the political progressive' (Wallace [1997] 2000, 68). Hardly a feminist haven for the women involved, what was extraordinary about the Push in the general conservatism of 1950s and early 1960s Australia was the acceptance of female sexual desire and women's right to initiate sexual activity with men. Interviewed by Anne Coombs for her history of the Push, Lynne Segal (also an early Push member) described this experience for the women involved and its importance for their understanding of women's liberation later in the sixties. 'That moment of sexual liberation was absolutely crucial to the origins of feminism and women's liberation,' Segal said. 'We had to see what it was like to be one of the boys, to be bachelor girls, who, just as men did, went for everything we wanted, and we did' (Coombs 1996, 129). This early experience of sexual independence and apparent sexual equality strongly influenced Greer, and was one element in the genesis of cuntpower.

The bequest of the Push discussions, readings and sexual lifestyle for Greer was a belief that freedoms enacted in one field, especially sexual, would extend to other sectors of life. The inspirations were Herbert Marcuse and Wilhelm Reich. In *Eros and Civilisation* ([1955] 1966) Marcuse had argued that under capitalism, sexuality had been repressed and this contributed to maintaining a more generalised repression, politically, and psychologically. From Reich's *The Sexual Revolution* ([1936] 1974) Greer retained the belief that unrepressed sexuality was a revolutionary force that could topple the patriarchal state and that full orgasm was the key to liberation.

Greer refused to settle for the clitoral orgasms of Masters and Johnson, 'the blueprint for standard, low-agitation, cool-out monogamy. If women are to avoid this last reduction of their humanity, they must hold out not just for orgasm but for ecstasy' ([1970c] 1999, 50). Of Anne Koedt's 'The Myth of the Vaginal Orgasm', Greer agreed that the focus on the vagina as the sole site for the female orgasm had made orgasm an unattainable goal for many women. But she argued instead that 'the substitution of the clitoral spasm for genuine gratification may turn out to be a disaster for sexuality ... the index of the desexualisation of the whole body' ([1970c] 1999, 48–49). Koedt's complete dismissal of the vagina as having a role in female sexual pleasure was a position Greer ridiculed: 'One wonders just whom Miss Koedt has gone to bed with' (345). Greer insisted that the vagina was not without the capacity to provide intense pleasure. In *The Female Eunuch* she wrote: 'It is nonsense to say that a woman feels nothing when a man is moving his penis in her vagina: the orgasm is qualitatively different when the vagina can undulate around the penis instead of vacancy' (48).

Instead, Greer developed her theory of cuntpower. 'The worst name anyone can be called is cunt' ([1970c] 1999, 44), she argued, thus justifying her reclamation of the term for women as a revolutionary battle cry. In the underground European sex newspaper *Suck* of which Greer was an editor, an article by 'Germaine' was entitled 'Lady Love your Cunt'. Here, Greer extolled the beauty and virtues of the cunt, including instructions on how to masturbate to orgasm, vaginally, without hands ([1970] 1986, 74–77). Greer reclaimed what had become a term of misogynistic abuse to refer to the whole genital area of the female, a potential opening to the as yet unknown erotic possibilities of the whole body.

Cuntpower was a heterosexual vision. And critically for the popular reception of Greer's ideas, her argument was that a liberated female sexuality would occur in *conjunction* with men—not without them. In her 1970 essay 'The Slag-heap Erupts' for the underground periodical OZ in London, Greer argued that rejecting men was akin to running the revolution from a nunnery, where some women might find independence 'but that never changed reality for the mass of women' (Greer [1970a] 1986, 28). 'While it is true that male–female relationships in our society are perverted, it is not a revolutionary solution to eschew all such contact', she argued in an article for the Australian magazine *Forum*, which specialised in journalism about sex (Greer 1974, 16). Greer was far from alone in her desire. Lynne Segal reminds us, 'the majority of feminists then believed that men could, and must, change. Women's personal struggle with the men in their lives was seen as the main aim of sexual politics in the early seventies' (1997, 16). Having sex with men became an active exploration to see what a liberated female sexuality—for women who identified as heterosexual—might look like. To do this, women had to pursue their own sexual liberation, not wait for men to tell them how.

Orgasm with a man, but achieved actively through a moving cunt, not passively bearing a man's weight, was Greer's ideal for the sexual liberation of women. It was an argument she made repeatedly. In her essay 'The Politics of Female Sexuality' for the 'Female Energy' issue of *OZ* magazine (also known as the 'Cuntpower issue'), for example:

> Once a woman throws her leg over her lover she has accepted responsibility for her own sexuality and recognized it as an integral part of her personality and her intelligence, and not merely a function of meat. Once she is posed over her lover, male or female, she is able not merely to claim the right of orgasm but espouse the sweet responsibility of giving pleasure. (1970b, 11)

In *The Female Eunuch*, for example:

> Men are tired of having all the responsibility for sex, it is time they were relieved of it. And I do not mean that large-scale lesbianism should be adopted, but simply that the emphasis should be taken off male genitality and replaced by human sexuality. The cunt must come into its own. (356)

Part of her cuntpower argument was that women could experience the positive power of actively giving pleasure to a man and in the flow of movement that *she* controlled, give pleasure to herself as well. Women had not only been denied the right to *receive* orgasm, their acculturated passivity had denied them the pleasure of *giving* orgasm. It is a fluid vision of heterosexual practice, where pleasure and power flow between male and female, active and passive, subject and object. Greer disarticulated the traditional binary couplings of penetration/activity and reception/passivity. 'Cunt is knowledge. Knowledge is receptivity, which is activity' (1970b, 10). Moreover, cuntpower radically offered a new conceptualisation of female genitalia which did not pit clitoris against vagina.

At the time, given the context of sexual conservatism, censorship, and ignorance within which most young Australians had been raised post-Second World War, the proposition that female heterosexuality was not necessarily or inherently passive was a radical vision. 'In the early 1970s sex was a topic which abounded in mythology', reflected Bettina Arndt, a sexual therapist at the time and editor of the Australian magazine *Forum*.

> Most people knew very little about sex and what they thought they knew was often wrong. It was widely assumed, for instance, that most women had very little interest in sex – and those who did were regarded as nymphomaniacs. Female orgasm had rarely been heard of and the clitoris was quite uncharted territory. (1982, 176)

Greer was throwing the widespread assumptions about the passive heterosexual woman into question. Greer had also pin-pointed one of the paradoxes and limitations of the feminist insistence on the supremacy of clitoral orgasm. For women who desired sex with men, once again men would become the masters of sexual pleasure, 'giving' women orgasms through their expert techniques of clitoral stimulation. 'Love-making has become another male skill, of which women are the judges,' wrote Greer ([1970c] 1999, 47). If heterosexual women actually wanted to involve their male partners in an orgasmic process by directing their attention only towards the clitoris, they would now be *more* reliant on male skill, not less. Unless women took responsibility for their own orgasms, men would remain in control.

The theory of cuntpower further worked to alienate Greer from the WLM, not just with her ideas about female orgasm and her sympathy for men, but with her criticisms of the movement itself.

> Revolutionary women may join Women's Liberation Groups and curse and scream and fight the cops but did you ever hear of one of them marching the public street with her skirt high crying 'Can you dig it? Cunt is beautiful!' (1970b, 10)

Through her journalism, her book, her media performances, however, Greer's diffuse statements about cuntpower also inspired many 'ordinary' women (as much as it terrified others), especially those who had not been involved in WLM or exposed to feminist reading lists, that more was possible in their heterosexual experiences. In her insistence that women take control of sexual acts with men, in the need for women's own knowledge about their bodies, in her refusal to limit orgasm just to the clitoris, it could be argued that more women came to understandings of their sexual and orgasmic potential than would have been the case without her. The sisters may have despaired, but ordinary women were fascinated. The figure of Greer became metonymic in the popular imagination for women's liberation and its connection to sexual freedom.

Glancing at Germaine

Germaine Greer's *The Female Eunuch* was released in Australia over the summer of 1971–1972, and Greer toured to promote the book with much media publicity (Lilburn, Magarey, and Sheridan 2000). Greer turned the characteristics that had defined the female castrate —'timidity, plumpness, languor, delicacy and preciosity'—on their heads, and enacted the opposite (Greer [1970c] 1999, 17). Her passionate arguments about the sexual liberation of women and her condemnation of the ordinary woman as complicit in her own oppression, 'galvanized many women, both feminist and non-feminist' against her (Spongberg 1993, 414). But it can also be argued that Greer was 'the most popularly influential feminist of the entire second wave, at least when it came to inspiring women's delinquency' (Wallace [1997] 2000, 284). Examining the press representations of Germaine Greer's tour in 1972, for example, Lilburn et al. found that Greer emerged 'as much a darling of the media as a critic of its sexist practices—and of the marginalization of women journalists' (2000, 29–30). While many would argue that this was due to the way the media had sexualised Greer to make feminism palatable (Genovese 2002, 156) and that Greer herself encouraged this treatment (Spongberg 1993), it could also be argued that Greer understood implicitly that feminism was going to be made in the media as much (or moreso) as outside it. As she said to journalist Sally Quinn for an interview with the *Washington Post* for her 1971 book tour of America,

> I'm a complete media freak. And the only reason I ever submitted to the commercialisation of Germaine Greer is to help women in the home, to raise the self-image of women, to spread the movement to the widest possible base. (quoted in Buchanan 2015; n/p)

As Chilla Bulbeck concluded after her interview-based research into the impact of the second wave on three generations of Australian women, '*The Female Eunuch* became almost synonymous with women's liberation, even as the growing handful of Australian feminists repudiated her work' (1997, 2). Many of Bulbeck's interview subjects mention Greer and *The Female Eunuch* as their stimulus to feminist awareness, as well, for some, as their reason for rejecting a feminist identity. Interviewees also referred to the *importance* of the media in providing that 'click' of recognition around the oppression of women.

In the pages of the new young women's magazine *Cleo* that launched in Australia in 1972, for example, Greer's name appears across the following decade like shorthand for feminism. One uncharacteristically hostile feature against women's liberation ran in February 1973, opening with the phrase 'Eat your heart out, Germaine Greer'. It gave voice to the women

> who are happy with their role, who enjoy being pampered and protected, who like the safe refuge of being cared for, who want to be wives and mothers and are happy to stay firmly feminine, retaining all the privileges it brings from men. (Nelson 1973, 112)

Entitled 'Strike One Against Women's Lib' the eruption of reactions from readers on the letters pages in coming months made sure there would be no strike two from *Cleo*. 'This article reveals an ignorance of the fundamental and basic issues of Women's Lib', wrote Lorraine Sidey of St Kilda, Vic. 'I think that before these women denounce Germaine Greer and other supporters they should become informed on the ideas involved' (April 1973, 146). Later in the decade, *Cleo* could run a story about how far women had come, grateful for the work of feminists like Greer.

> ... slowly, slowly, lots of women are beginning to enjoy their femaleness without at the same time reining it in to conform to some fantasy version of femininity ... Maybe Women's Lib has raised my consciousness; maybe it would have happened in any case ... I'm no rebel. I like to feel accepted. Other women (Germaine Greer, I love you) cleared the way. (Knight 1977, 84)

Greer's media presence could be read as a series of 'glances'. She was a 'political bonehead' and 'ideologically inconsistent' according to Beatrice Faust (Faust 1972, 1), however a coherent political platform was not Greer's aim. Her aim was to inspire women to revolt. And many women 'read' Greer via her media moments and not through an extended examination of her writings. It is a highly intellectual and rational understanding of the world and of how the media operates to assume that influence and ideas can only spread through a logical and ordered reading process. Greer's meaning was made through 'a performative and dramatic pedagogy, visual and vestimentary, and its message—precisely because it is not spelt out but performed as part of popular entertainment—can be read "at a glance"' (Hartley 1996, 181). What John Hartley terms the 'logic of the glance' is one of the ways in which meaning is constructed through media and celebrity, and it helps to explain Greer *as* the meaning of women's liberation for women who were still trying to work out what feminism might be and how they could 'live' the desire for gender equality and for orgasmic sex in everyday heterosexual lives. Greer's popular performances of sexual liberation, the anecdotes about her sex life, are what many women remember about women's liberation. As Sybil Nolan writes:

> There was an element of recklessness in Greer's performance that women admired and men found sexy. 'How could she dare say that?' we wondered. 'How could she risk doing that?' The corollary was to ask what we ourselves could say or do. (1999, 169)

Greer was a woman prepared to put her reputation on the line—indeed to make her reputation—through dirty talk and an overt heterosexuality. She was not a man-hater, although she gave men much grief. The message at a glance was that one of the steps to women liberating themselves had to be through sex with men, not without them. And women had to be active—desiring sex, initiating sex, controlling its movement to make penetration a female activity and orgasm an experience they were in charge of. This was a kind of liberatory practice ordinary women could embrace. It sounded like something you might be able to manage in your own bedroom. And you did not have to join the local chapter of the WLM to achieve it. As Marilyn Lake argues, there was a 'tension' between the aim of Women's Liberation to create a mass movement and the sense of alienation many women felt from the 'Libbers style, presentation, and language, 'an "us" and "them" attitude which left suburban women feeling threatened' (1999, 236). In her autobiography, *Ducks on the Pond*, Anne Summers wrote of the exclusivity of Sydney Women's Liberation. 'In theory ... open to any woman, in practice the group was very picky ... They admitted into their group only women like themselves: young, educated, inner city' (1999, 298). Part of Greer's appeal was her insistence on personal rebellion. It was a tactic that even the most ordinary woman could find inspiring: 'The first exercise of the free woman is to devise her own mode of revolt [reflecting] her own independence and originality' ([1970c] 1999, 20). Indeed, Summers describes *The Female Eunuch* as the book 'so-called ordinary women read' as distinct from the 'more radical tomes' written and read by those in the movement (1999, 298). Greer herself appreciated the realities of life for the ordinary woman. If not always sympathetic, and often scathing about women's complicity in their own oppression, Greer also understood that it was through mediated outrage and shock that feminist ideas might begin to take hold. In 'The slagheap erupts', Greer showed her usual mix of disdain and insight:

> The average housewife is dulled and confused by her day-to-day diet of pulp journalism and crap television ... Of course, most women are not radical leftists or unmarried university students; the luxury of [such] theorizing is not accessible to them at all. Mrs Smith, who tends a

bottling machine by day and husband and kids morning and night, has no use for a reading list, however fascinating. ([1970a] 1986, 27)

The ordinary woman may not have been reading feminist theory but she was tuned in to the media and she was having sex. To discover what pleasures a female body was capable of, was a 'liberation' of a kind. There was an embodied experience of equality to be struggled for there, especially via orgasm.

The ubiquity of Greer's presence in Australian media at the time ensured that some version of feminist ideas, and especially around the sexual liberation of women, were up for popular debate. As Lilburn et al. conclude, 'Her presence challenged media representations of women and thus disrupted cultural meanings normally associated with "woman" ... [opening up] a public space in which feminist ideas could be discussed' (2000, 336). Anne Summers reflected that Greer 'opened eyes and changed lives. The book received enormous media coverage and thus got many thousands of women who might otherwise never (or at least not as soon) have been confronted with these truths about their lives' (1999, 293). Greer also cemented the conflation of the liberation of women with sexual liberation in the popular imagination, at a time when more radical feminists were starting to question heterosexuality itself under patriarchy and the early connection between women's and sexual liberation was breaking down.

Greer was aware of this, aware that her continued insistence on the importance of sexual liberation for the liberation of women was not approved of by many in the women's movement. In an interview with an un-named journalist for the underground periodical *SCREW: The Sex Review* in May 1971, re-printed in *SUCK* with the title 'I Am A Whore', Greer said:

> There's a big cleft between sexual liberation and woman's liberation. My sisters get mad at me ... they want me to wear pants and be unavailable, and carry a jimmy to bash people over the head with if they feel my ass in the street. They get mad at me for calling myself superwhore, supergroupie, and all that stuff. They think I'm cheapening myself, I'm allowing people to laugh at me, when the whole point is that if my body is sacred and mine to dispose of, then I don't have to build things around it like it was property that could be stolen. (n/d, n/p)

Greer was also aware that her constant presence in the media was a thorn in the side of a woman's movement that wanted no leaders or stars. More radical feminists at the time did not see the mainstream media as a space where feminism might indeed be made rather than just (mis)represented. While the mass media was recognised as being enormously important in the socialisation of women, for many feminists of the second wave co-operating with or writing for the commercial 'mass media' was like sleeping with the enemy. Margaret Jones, a journalist for the Australian left-leaning weekly *The National Times*, wrote about the 'paranoia' of the women's movement when it came to the mainstream press:

> One of the dilemmas of the women's movement today [is that] the sisters long to express their points of view and to proselytise but are too suspicious of the orthodox media of communication to allow free reportage. (Jones 1973, 14)

Closed sessions at the Women's Commission of 1973 made even potentially positive coverage via *The National Times* impossible. Jones concluded that the movement was in danger of only 'preaching to the converted and remaining caged within their own elitist circles'. Greer had pointed out at the time how this strategy was backfiring. True to her anarchist-libertarian background, Greer regarded a boycott of the mass media as a form of inverse censorship. As a journalist–provocateur she wrote for the underground periodicals *Oz* and *Suck*, and for more mainstream publications such as the *Sunday Review*, *Sunday Times*, *Playboy*, *Esquire*, *Harper's*. In Australia wrote for *Forum* and edited the re-launch issue of the style and culture magazine *Pol* (May 1972) and was interviewed internationally for newspapers, magazine, radio and television. Greer distanced herself from many other radical feminists by choosing the strategy of hoisting the mass media 'on its own petard':

> After the first rush of derisive publicity women's liberation has adopted a suspicious and uncooperative attitude to the press, a tactic which has in no way improved their public image or even protected it from figuring so large in Sunday supplements and glossy magazines. In fact, no publicity is still bad publicity … It is to be hoped that more and more women decide to influence the media by writing for them, not being written about … In any case, insulting and excluding reporters is no defence against them; censorship is the weapon of oppression, not ours. ([1970c] 1999, 348)

When it came to dealing with the media, the more radical members of the second wave were caught in a bind of their own making. It is a contradiction that Rita Felski explores in *Beyond Feminist Aesthetics*. Within the movement, the desire for a gender-specific identity and for feminist women 'to define themselves against the homogenizing and universalizing logic of the global megaculture of modern mass communication' created a feminist counter-public sphere in the 1960s and 1970s (1989, 166). But because second wave feminism wanted to speak for all women, because it contained universalising tendencies, 'the feminist public sphere also constitutes a discursive arena which disseminates its arguments outwards through such public channels of communication as books, journals, the mass media, and the education system' (168). It was a contradiction that Greer innately understood and refused to be caught up in. She may have been alienated from much of the feminist movement, and criticised harshly, but the price she paid was an influential popularity amongst ordinary women ensuring that within popular understandings of feminism, sexual, and women's liberation remained entwined.

Conclusion

The original title of this article was 'Exhuming Germaine's Theory of Cuntpower'. Exhumation brings a lifeless body to the surface for examination but does not give it life. The theory of cuntpower has been ignored by scholars, buried in an unmarked grave. It does not figure in the histories of second wave sexual politics. But is there any life to be found in the corpse of this concept?

Greer herself would now say no. Decades after the writings explored above, Greer recanted. In her 1999 book *The Whole Woman*, Greer mounted arguments against penetrative sex that sounded remarkably like Anne Koedt, and a little like Andrea Dworkin. The only sexuality that had been freed was male sexuality 'which is fixated on penetration' (6). 'Penetration equals domination in the animal world and therefore in the unregenerate human world which is part of it. The penetree, regardless of sex, cannot rule, OK?' (6).

> A woman's pleasure is not dependent upon the presence of a penis in the vagina; neither is a man's. We must ask therefore why intromission is still, perhaps more than ever, described as

normal or full intercourse ... The explanation seems to lie in the symbolic nature of intercourse as an act of domination. (89)

To hold Greer to account for departing so dramatically from her earlier beliefs is unfair. She is a scholar and a public intellectual who is allowed to change her mind. In fact, she should be praised for doing so, whether we agree with her new pronouncements or not. What interests me more is whether there is any usefulness now, beyond historical antiquarianism, in the idea of cuntpower. At a time when many queer theorists refute the association of orgasm with political transformation, Greer's ideas seem almost daft or at least hopelessly out of date. As Annamarie Jagose writes 'the long-standing but increasingly implausible connection between orgasm and political transformation depends on a liberationist understanding of power that queer theory foundationally refutes' (2013, 11–12).

And yet ... As this article has argued, Greer's exhortations to ordinary women to learn about their bodies, to take control of the act of vaginal penetration, to actively find their own way to sexual pleasure, to demand their right to orgasm, was socially powerful, although certainly limited by its focus on heterosex. Greer's overwhelming presence in the media of the time and her insistence that women's liberation was enmeshed with sexual liberation is part of the genealogy behind a leitmotif of popular media and culture in the decades that followed, from *Cleo* and *Cosmopolitan* magazines to *Sex and the City* and some strands of postfeminism. Cuntpower had an afterlife, in attitude if not in name. While cuntpower may not have brought about the release of energy necessary for the revolution Greer had hoped for, at a personal level for many women in their everyday sexual lives there was indeed a transformation that could be considered 'political'. And at a time when women are still struggling for their sexual rights—to orgasm, to sex without shame, to sex without judgement, to sex without violence—perhaps there is still life to be found in this body of Greer's work.

Notes

1. Although Greer's first use of the term cuntpower appears in an unpublished letter to Australian Prime Minister John Gorton in 1969, the text is only available (to my knowledge) in Greer's collection of essays and occasional writings *The Madwoman's Underclothes* (1986). In this publication cuntpower is referred to as 'cunt-power' and as two separate words 'cunt' 'power'. In this article I am following the usage that appears in the 'Female Energy' issue of *OZ* magazine 29 (London) where cuntpower is used as one word. Germaine Greer was closely involved with its production along with Jim Anderson, Gary Brayley, Felix Dennis, Richard Neville, Bruce Sawford, and Liz Watson. Detective Inspector Luff is also acknowledged for his 'help'. Although the cover describes the issue as 'Female Energy OZ', the inside editorial letter describes it as 'Cuntpower OZ'. This issue was one month late due to the editorial office having been raided by Scotland Yard's Obscenity Squad. The editors decided not to further inflame the censors by putting the word cuntpower on the cover.
2. Carmichael was the leader of the US Student Nonviolent Co-ordination Committee.
3. See the edited collection by Vance (1984), *Pleasure and Danger: Exploring Female Sexuality*, for a clear elaboration of the state of the 'sex wars' at this time.

References

Albury, Kath. 2002. *Yes Means Yes. Getting Explicit about Heterosex*. Crows Nest: Allen & Unwin.
Arndt, Bettina. 1982. "Did the Earth Move for You? 10 Years that Shook the Bedrooms of the World." *Cleo*, November, 176–179.
Buchanan, Rachel. 2015. "Life of the Party." *Pursuit*. https://pursuit.unimelb.edu.au/articles/life-of-the-party.
Bulbeck, Chilla. 1997. *Living Feminism: The Impact of the Women's Movement on Three Generations of Australian Women*. Cambridge: Cambridge University Press.
Coombs, Anne. 1996. *Sex and Anarchy. The Life and Death of the Sydney Push*. Melbourne: Penguin.
Coote, Anna, and Beatrix Campbell. 1982. *Sweet Freedom: The Struggle for Women's Liberation*. Oxford: Basil Blackwell.
Curthoys, Ann. 1992. "Doing it for Themselves. The Women's Movement since 1970." In *Gender relations in Australia. Domination and negotiation*, edited by Kay Saunders, and Raymond Evans, 425–447. Marrickville: Harcourt, Brace Jovanovich.
Dimen, Muriel. 1984. "Politically Correct? Politically Incorrect?" In *Pleasure and Danger: Exploring Female Sexuality*, edited by Carole S. Vance, 131–148. Boston, MA: Routledge & Kegan Paul.
Echols, Alice. 1989. *Daring to be Bad. Radical Feminism in America 1967–1975*. Minneapolis: University of Minnesota Press.
English, Deirdre, Amber Hollibaugh, and Gayle Rubin. 1982. "Talking Sex: A Conversation on Sexuality and Feminism." *Feminist Review* 11 (1): 40–52.
Faust, Beatrice. 1972. "Dr Greer and the Eunuch." *The Australian Humanist*, March 21, 1.
Felski, Rita. 1989. *Beyond Feminist Aesthetics: Feminist Literature and Social Change*. Cambridge, MA: Harvard University Press.
'Gale'. 1971. "Review of an ABZ of Love." *Mejane* March, 13.
Gallop, Jane. 1997. *Feminist Accused of Sexual Harassment*. Durham, NC: Duke University Press.
Garton, Stephen. 2004. *Histories of Sexuality*. London: Equinox.
Genovese, Ann. 2002. "Madonna and/or Whore? Feminism(s) and Public Sphere(s)." In *Romancing the Tomes. Popular Culture, Law and Feminism*, edited by Margaret Thornton, 147–164. London: Cavendish.
Gerhard, Jane. 2000. "Revisiting 'The Myth of the Vaginal Orgasm': The Female Orgasm in America Sexual Thought." *Feminist Studies* 26 (2): 440–476.
Gerhard, Jane. 2001. *Desiring Revolution: Second-wave Feminism and the Rewriting of American Sexual Thought, 1920 to 1982*. New York, NY: Columbia University Press.
Greer, Germaine. (1970) 1986. "Lady Love your Cunt." In *The Madwoman's Underclothes. Essays and Occasional Writings 1968–1985*, edited by Germaine Greer, 74–77. Suffolk: Picador.
Greer, Germaine. (1970a) 1986. "The Slagheap Erupts." In *The Madwoman's Underclothes. Essays and Occasional Writings 1968–1985*, edited by Germaine Greer, 25–29. Suffolk: Picador.
Greer, Germaine. 1970b. "The Politics of Female Sexuality." *OZ (London)* 29: 10–11.
Greer, Germaine. (1970c) 1999. *The Female Eunuch*. London: Flamingo.
Greer, Germaine. 1974. "Inside Germaine Greer." *Forum* 2 (5): 12–16.
Greer, Germaine. (No date). "I am a Whore." *Suck* 6, n/p.
Hartley, John. 1996. *Popular Reality. Journalism, Modernity, Popular Culture*. London: Arnold.
Jagose, Annamarie. 2013. *Orgasmology*. Durham, NC: Duke University Press.
Jones, Margaret. 1973. "Paranoia: The New Bar to Liberation." *The National Times* March 26–31, 14.
Knight, Rachel. 1977. "It's Great to be a Woman in 1977." *Cleo*, April, 84–87.
Koedt, Anne. (1970) 1973. "The Myth of the Vaginal Orgasm." In *Radical Feminism*, edited by Anne Koedt, Ellen Levine, and Anita Rapone, 198–207. New York, NY: Quadrangle Books.
Lake, Marilyn. 1999. *Getting Equal. The History of Australian Feminism*. Sydney: Allen & Unwin.

Lilburn, Sandra, Susan Magarey, and Susan Sheridan. 2000. "Celebrity Feminism as Synthesis: Germaine Greer, The Female Eunuch and the Australian Print Media." *Continuum: Journal of Media & Cultural Studies* 14 (3): 335–348.

Marcuse, Herbert. (1955) 1966. *Eros and Civilisation: A Philosophical Inquiry into Freud*. Boston, MA: Beacon Press.

Masters, William H., and Virginia Johnson. 1966. *Human Sexual Response*. Toronto: Bantam Books.

Matthews, Jill Julius. 1997. "Introduction." In *Sex in Public. Australian Sexual Cultures*, edited by Jill Julius Mathews, i–xiii. St Leonards: Allen & Unwin.

Nelson, Angela. 1973. "Strike One Against Women's Lib." *Cleo*, February, 112–113.

Nolan, Sybil. 1999. "Tabloid Women." *Meanjin* 2: 165–177.

Reich, Wilhelm. (1936) 1974. *The Sexual Revolution* (Translated by Therese Pol). New York, NY: Farrar, Strauss and Giroux.

Segal, Lynne. 1994. *Straight Sex. The Politics of Pleasure*. London: Virago.

Segal, Lynne. 1997. *New Sexual Agendas*. Basingstoke: Macmillan.

Smart, Carol. 1996. "Collusion, Collaboration and Confession: On Moving Beyond the Heterosexuality Debate." In *Theorising Heterosexuality. Telling it Straight*, edited by Diane Richardson, 161–178. Buckingham: Open University Press.

Snitow, Ann. 1989. "Pages from a Gender Diary: Basic Divisions in Feminism." *Dissent* 36 (2): 205–224.

Spongberg, Mary. 1993. "If She's so Great, How Some so Many Pigs Dig Her? Germaine Greer and the Malestream Press." *Women's History Review* 2 (3): 407–419.

Summers, Anne. 1999. *Ducks on the Pond*. Ringwood: Penguin.

Vance, Carole S. 1984. *Pleasure and Danger: Exploring Female Sexuality*. Boston, MA: Routledge & Kegan Paul.

Wallace, Christine. (1997) 2000. *Germaine Greer. Untamed Shrew*. London: Richard Cohen Books.

Willis, Ellen. 1994. "Villains and Victims: 'Sexual Correctness' and the Repression of Feminism." In *Bad Girls, Good Girls. Women, Sex and Power in the Nineties*, edited by Nan Bauer Maglin, and Donna Perry, 44–53. New Brunswick, NJ: Rutgers University Press.

Germaine Greer's 'arch enemy': Arianna Stassinopoulos' 1974 Australian tour

Isobelle Barrett Meyering

ABSTRACT

In 1973, Arianna Stassinopoulos published her anti-feminist tract, *The Female Woman*. Specifically formulated and marketed as a response to Germaine Greer's *The Female Eunuch* (1970), the book went on to become one of the bestselling backlash texts of the 1970s. This article examines the impact of this opposition on popular understandings of Greer and second-wave feminism, through a case study of media coverage of Stassinopoulos' visit to Australia in November 1974. Although *The Female Woman* capitalised on Greer's celebrity for the purposes of backlash politics and Stassinopoulos' own career, I argue that its invocation of Greer ultimately served to extend the mainstream media's engagement with feminism. While one effect of the book and the publicity around it was to perpetuate a view of Greer as synonymous with women's liberation, media coverage of the tour also helped to extend discussion about the nature of leadership and representation in feminist politics. Furthermore, Greer's own popularity proved to be a key factor militating against Stassinopoulos' appeal. In this instance, Greer's celebrity – the very quality that Stassinopoulos sought to exploit for her own benefit – served as a powerful countervailing force to anti-feminism, moderating the traction that Stassinopoulos was able to achieve.

Introduction

On 5 November 1973, *The Sydney Morning Herald*'s London correspondent Lynne Bell reported in the newspaper's social pages on the publication of Greek-born and Cambridge-educated Arianna Stassinopoulos' book, *The Female Woman* (1973). 'If you are the type who runs screaming at the mention of Women's Lib, then Arianna Stassinopoulos is your girl … [She] has come to your rescue with "The Female Woman" – a downright challenge to "The Female Eunuch"', Bell declared ('Salvo at forces of liberation', *The Sydney Morning Herald*, November 5, 1973). Almost exactly one year later, on 15 November 1974, Stassinopoulos arrived in Australia for a two-week promotional tour, starting in Sydney. In the lead up to and during the visit, Stassinopoulos was routinely referred to as Greer's major rival in Britain, indeed, her 'arch enemy' ('Women's Lib all Greek to her', *The Age,* November 16, 1974; 'Sylvia's woman to women: It's been a good week', *Sunday*

Mail, November 24, 1974). By the end of the tour, a clear narrative had been established around Stassinopoulos and Greer as not just intellectual but personal adversaries.

Stassinopoulos is now better known to us as Arianna Huffington, co-founder and editor-in-chief of *The Huffington Post*. Born in Athens in July 1950, the daughter of a well-off Greek economist, she moved to England to study at Cambridge University. She first came to public attention in 1971 when she was elected president of the prestigious Cambridge Union Society, only the third woman to ever be appointed to the position. With the publication of *The Female Woman*, one of the first book-length responses to the new feminist movement,[1] she established her reputation as a political conservative, later marrying Republican Michael Huffington (they divorced in 1997). After decades as a right-wing commentator, she switched to the progressive side of politics in the 2000s ('The oracle: the many lives of Arianna Huffington', *The New Yorker*, October 13, 2008). She had come a long way from her days as a leading spokesperson for the anti-feminist cause.

Given her media profile, it is somewhat surprising that Stassinopoulos has so far received little attention from scholars concerned with the trajectory of Anglo-American second-wave feminism and the backlash against it that would gather greater momentum in the late 1970s and 1980s (Faludi 1992; Rowland 1984; Tyler 2007).[2] One reason for this oversight is that Stassinopoulos did not develop close connections with any single organisation during this period, although her work was cited by anti-feminist groups, including in Australia. In addition, Stassinopoulos' somewhat idiosyncratic politics make her difficult to place as a backlash figure. On the one hand, like other anti-feminist texts of the period, *The Female Woman* reasserted 'innate' biological difference as the basis for social organisation, emphasised women's 'natural' maternal desires and defended marriage and the nuclear family. On the other hand, Stassinopoulos presented herself as a moderate figure, continually emphasising that she was not opposed to 'equality', but simply in favour of 'choice'; moreover, she expressed relatively liberal views on birth control and homosexual law reform. This makes it harder to place Stassinopoulos than her contemporaries such as Anita Bryant, Midge Decter, Phyllis Schlafly and Mary Whitehouse.

While *The Female Woman* clearly warrants further critical attention for this distinctive contribution to the anti-feminist backlash, my own focus in this article is a narrower one. As underlined above by *The Sydney Morning Herald*'s London correspondent, Stassinopoulos' book was not simply a response to the emergence of women's liberation but was formulated and marketed specifically as a response to *The Female Eunuch* (1970) and it is this conscious attempt to use Greer for the purposes of backlash politics that is my central concern here. Specifically, this article examines Stassinopoulos' use of Greer as a cultural symbol of women's liberation through a case study of the media coverage in the lead up to and during her visit to Australia in November 1974. I argue that Stassinopoulos capitalised on Greer's celebrity for the purposes of backlash politics and her own career, but that her invocation of Greer nonetheless served to extend the mainstream media's engagement with feminism. Using Greer in this way had a range of implications for popular understandings of Greer. On the one hand, it built on and helped to perpetuate a view of Greer as synonymous with women's liberation, despite feminist objections that the two were not the same (Spongberg 1993; Wallace 1997). At the same time, media coverage around the book also served to extend discussion about what exactly Greer (and women's liberation more generally) stood for. As such, the tour provides a gauge of Greer's own popularity at this point and her capacity to serve as a countervailing force to anti-feminism, while also serving as a valuable lens onto the feminist politics of leadership and representation at this time.

The article explores these concerns firstly by providing an overview of *The Female Woman* as a response to Greer's *The Female Eunuch*, before moving to focus on the Australian tour. The analysis presented is based on a survey of articles published in November 1974 in a selection of daily newspapers: *The Advertiser* (Adelaide), *The Age* (Melbourne), *The Australian* (national), *The Canberra Times* (Canberra), *The Courier-Mail* (Brisbane) and *The Sydney Morning Herald* (Sydney).[3] I also include articles on Stassinopoulos published in 1974 in the country's two leading women's magazines, *The Australian Women's Weekly* and *Woman's Day*, as well as *Cleo*, a new magazine that was openly sympathetic to the feminist cause and the first to give significant coverage to Stassinopoulos. Drawing on these sources, I assess to what extent Stassinopoulos was able to capitalise on Greer's celebrity to promote her anti-feminist position during the tour, the role of local feminist responses in complicating Stassinopoulos' representation of Greer and, finally, how Stassinopoulos' own appeal was dependent on and moderated by Greer and feminism's wider appeal.

(Mis)representing Greer and women's liberation in *The Female Woman*

In the wake of the publication of *The Female Eunuch*, Greer emerged as one of the best-known figures of women's liberation; indeed, as the first 'celebrity feminist' (Lilburn, Magarey, and Sheridan 2000; Taylor 2014). This also made Greer a prime target for backlash politics, as Stassinopoulos well understood when she began writing *The Female Woman*. From the time of its inception, the book was formulated as a response to Greer's bestseller. The original idea was conceived in 1971, during the very early days of Greer's publishing success, while Stassinopoulos was still president of the Cambridge Union Society. Soon after her election to the position of president, she gave a number of press interviews on the subject of women's liberation. She claimed that she was subsequently approached by Greer's own publisher, who proposed that she write a rejoinder to *The Female Eunuch*. By the end of her term as president, Stassinopoulos had written a draft and decided on the title ('The delightful Miss Arianna Stassinopoulos', *The Times*, November 29, 1971). She was already spruiking its key argument: her distinction between 'liberation' and 'emancipation'. 'Liberation', as advocated by the likes of Greer, required the elimination of all differences between men and women, Stassinopoulos asserted; 'emancipation', by contrast, involved giving 'equal status' to 'distinctively female roles', especially that of wife and mother ('The delightful Miss Arianna Stassinopoulos'; Stassinopoulos 1974, 15).

Upon publication in 1973, the title made *The Female Woman* instantly recognisable as a riposte to Greer's bestseller and the marketing campaign in Britain invited a comparison between the two figures, setting up a pattern that would be repeated in the Australian coverage. For example, an early book review in *The Times* continued the line that *The Female Woman* was a response to *The Female Eunuch* ('Ideas about the sexes', *The Times*, November 1, 1973), while *The Observer* published an excerpt from the book accompanied by images of Stassinopoulos, Greer and Kate Millett ('Vive la difference!', *The Observer*, October 28, 1973). The marketing of the book as a response to *The Female Eunuch* also forced Greer herself to respond ('The errors of Arianna', *The Listener*, November

15, 1973), a fact on which Stassinopoulos' publishers capitalised. The back cover of the paperback edition, released in 1974, featured a quote from a defiant Greer, asserting that 'Miss Stassinopoulos hopes that her book will destroy the Women's Liberation movement ... but the withers of the movement are unwrung'. That Greer had even acknowledged Stassinopoulos was presented somewhat perversely here as further endorsement of the book.

Despite the publicity generated by *The Female Woman* not only for Stassinopoulos but also for Greer, it has largely been neglected by scholars interested in Greer's status as a feminist figurehead. While Greer's own use of the media in this period has been well examined (Bradley 2003, 137–142; Le Masurier 2007a, 118–119; Lilburn, Magarey, and Sheridan 2000; Spongberg 1993), the role of Stassinopoulos' *The Female Woman* in further shaping Greer's public profile at this time has yet to receive serious consideration. The treatment given to the book by Greer's biographer, Wallace (1997, 203), is especially telling: she devotes just one line to Stassinopoulos' book as part of a wider discussion of responses to *The Female Eunuch*, largely dismissing its value for understanding Greer on the basis that it 'was essentially a vehicle for anti-feminist backlash'. In so far as Stassinopoulos' book often deliberately misrepresented Greer's arguments, Wallace's response is understandable; certainly, we should approach *The Female Woman* cautiously as an analysis of Greer's ideas. Nonetheless, the book's impact on popular understandings of Greer's relationship to feminism was considerable and warrants further analysis.

Close examination of the text of *The Female Woman* is illuminating in terms of understanding why Stassinopoulos chose to focus on Greer. While many of the big names of women's liberation were mentioned in the book, Greer was referenced more frequently than any other figure; the index records 38 page references to Greer, more than double that for Millett, who was the next most discussed.[4] The importance of Greer was made most explicit in one of the final chapters of the book, entitled 'The Liberated Woman? ... And Her Liberators', in which Stassinopoulos set out to establish the 'elitist' nature of women's liberation. Here, Greer was specifically nominated as the movement's foremost leader. By virtue of her celebrity status, Greer was the definitive representative of women's liberation, Stassinopoulos argued. 'Women's liberation has become a cult that only expresses itself through the person of whoever happens to be the current "liberated" celebrity. Germaine Greer is Women's Lib – the cult figure is the movement', she asserted (Stassinopoulos 1974, 140).

Stassinopoulos' identification of Greer's celebrity as performing a particular function in relation to feminism – namely, that of providing a 'cult figure' for others to follow – is significant in understanding the way she positioned herself in the book. The idea that women's liberation was an 'elite' movement, comprising Greer and her followers, connected to Stassinopoulos' representation of women's liberation as a 'fashionable' cause. In *The Female Woman*, women's liberation was constructed as the new hegemony, while Stassinopoulos was positioned as the heroic opponent of the latest trend. Framing her book as a response to Greer made it easier to sustain this argument, as Greer was, indeed, 'fashionable', having been embraced by magazines ranging from *Life* to *Vogue*, where she was presented as a chic figure ('Germaine Greer', *LIFE*, May 7, 1971; 'Germaine Greer talks with Kathleen Tynan', *Vogue*, January 1, 1972). In this respect, it was also important for Stassinopoulos' case that Greer could be understood to be representative of the mainstream of women's liberation, rather than one of the 'really way-out extremists' such as radical feminist Valerie Solanas, author of the 'SCUM Manifesto' (1968) (Stassinopoulos 1974, 140–141).

Part of the attraction of Greer was also the fact that her personality, not just her ideas, had become a feature of popular discourse; indeed this is what marked Greer as one of the earliest feminist celebrities (Lilburn, Magarey, and Sheridan 2000). One of the main lines of attack that Stassinopoulos deployed against Greer, but not to the same extent against other figures such as Millett, was to accuse her of projecting her own experiences onto other women. This tactic was used most successfully in the critique of Greer's sexual relationships and her childhood, two areas that had become the subject of intense media speculation by the time *The Female Woman* was published. The chapter, 'The Sexual Woman', ended with a brief but pointed allusion to Greer's unsuccessful marriage, which, Stassinopoulos (1974, 57) reasoned, 'makes it easier to understand why she derides and ridicules so viciously the romantic myth which she regards as the centrepiece of feminine culture'. The attack on Greer's personal life continued in the next chapter, 'The Family Woman', in which Stassinpoulos sought to discredit Greer's critique of the nuclear family as skewed as a result of her own 'unhappy' childhood (60–61). Ironically it was the same quality that arguably made Greer resonate with many readers of *The Female Eunuch* – her use of her personal experience – that was exploited by Stassinopoulos in her case against her. Crucially, these attacks personalised the rivalry between Stassinopoulos and Greer, as well as contributing to a picture of Greer as the ultimate symbol of feminism's irrelevance to the 'average' woman. Greer was presented as an exceptional and somewhat pathological figure whose life experience distinguished her from other women, while Stassinopoulos emerged as more attuned to the desires of 'real' women.

Stassinopoulos' simple equation of Greer's celebrity with her status as the 'leader' of women's liberation was, of course, highly problematic. As has been well documented, the question of Greer's capacity to represent women's liberation was a subject of considerable contention among activists in Britain, the United States and Australia during this period (Bradley 2003; Lilburn, Magarey, and Sheridan 2000; Spongberg 1993; Wallace 1997). This is not to say that women's liberationists did not take Greer seriously. For example, *The Female Eunuch* was widely read and discussed in the Australian movement, particularly before other works became more widely available;[5] furthermore, during Greer's tour in 1971–1972, women's liberationists turned out to support her at multiple public engagements.[6] However, Greer was undoubtedly a controversial figure within women's liberation and by no means seen as representative of the movement as a whole. The idea that Greer or any single figure could represent the movement – or indeed that there was any single line on women's liberation – was fundamentally at odds with the movement's commitment to anti-hierarchical forms of organisation, that is, 'structurelessness'.

Yet, while Stassinopoulos' designation of Greer as synonymous with women's liberation was clearly a misrepresentation of the movement, she was not entirely misguided in her assessment of Greer's role as a celebrity feminist. Indeed, Stassinopoulos' text suggested at least some awareness of debates within women's liberation around the politics of 'structurelessness' and the problem of 'movement stars', most famously identified in American radical feminist Jo Freeman's classic essay 'The Tyranny of Structurelessness' (1972–1973).[7] In the same chapter in which she described Greer as a 'cult figure', Stassinopoulos (1974, 140) appropriated these very arguments for the purposes of her attack on women's liberation, asserting that, in their efforts to avoid hierarchy, the movement had itself 'succumbed to the tyranny of charismatic leadership' exemplified by Greer. Moreover, despite her claims about Greer's status as a 'cult figure' or 'leader' of women's liberation, Stassinopoulos clearly understood that the two were not in fact equivalent. Where convenient, she herself played off the idea that Greer was an aberration within women's liberation, highlighting Greer's own public denigration of other feminists and identifying grassroots activists' as being 'resentful' of the 'excessive prominence' of Greer (Stassinopoulos 1974, 140).

At stake here were fundamental questions relating to the feminist politics of leadership and representation. Stassinopoulos' insight into these issues distinguished *The Female Woman* from much of the other popular writing on Greer that equated her to women's liberation with little reference to the concerns of movement activists. Crucially, however, these nuances were glossed over by Stassinopoulos herself in the majority of the book and this acknowledgement of Greer's tenuous position within women's liberation was ultimately subordinated to Stassinopoulos' claims about her cult status. Similarly, these nuances were often lost in the media coverage of Stassinopoulos during her Australian tour. However, as the following discussion will show, the equation of Greer with women's liberation did not go uncontested, nor did it always serve Stassinopoulos in the way she hoped.

Stassinopoulos and the Australian media

By the time Stassinopoulos visited Australia in November 1974, she had emerged as a leading spokesperson for the anti-feminist cause and her rivalry with Greer was well-established. Stassinopoulos' visit formed part of an international book publicity exercise. She arrived on 15 November immediately following a visit to the United States, during which she had visited 28 cities, and she planned to spend three days in New Zealand on route back to England. Her arrival in Sydney made the front page of *The Sydney Morning Herald*, a sign of the high-profile media attention to come ('Women's Lib's worst friend: a hefty swipe at Germaine', *The Sydney Morning Herald*, November 16, 1974). At the end of the tour, one commentator would describe the coverage as having been 'ecstatic' ('A defence of the victors', *The Canberra Times*, November 29, 1974). But while the visit itself was crucial in establishing Stassinopoulos as a national news story, there had been a gradual build up to this moment, with women's magazines paving the way for coverage in the daily newspapers.

Publicity for Stassinopoulos' book in Australia had in fact begun in February 1974, when *Cleo* featured a three-page excerpt from the book. *Cleo* was a new magazine, first launched in November 1972, and had offered qualified support to women's liberation ('Welcome to Cleo', *Cleo*, November, 1972; Le Masurier 2007a, 2007b). More in tune with feminist debates and literature overseas, *Cleo* was significantly ahead of other media outlets in providing a platform to Stassinopoulos. The inclusion of the excerpt in the first instance was not, however, necessarily indicative of endorsement of *The Female Woman*. Indeed, perhaps anticipating objections from readers, the excerpt had come with a warning from editor Ita Buttrose that Stassinopoulos' views were 'easily more controversial' than women's liberation ('This month', *Cleo*, February, 1974). As media scholar Le Masurier (2007b, 201) has previously noted, *Cleo*'s decision to publish the excerpt from

Stassinopoulos' book provoked a sharp response from some readers and *Cleo* subsequently published a letter and then two-page reply by Melbourne women's liberationist Judy Gemmel.[8]

It took some time for Stassinopoulos to be discovered by the more established women's magazines. However, in the weeks leading up to the visit, they too took note of Stassinopoulos as a leading anti-feminist figure. On 16 October 1974, a month before her visit, *The Australian Women's Weekly*, the country's leading women's magazine, ran a full-page profile piece on Stassinopoulos, written by London reporter Camilla Beach ('Arianna's gunning for you, Germaine'). The magazine specifically invited readers to send them their views on Stassinopoulos and a full page of letters featured in the magazine three weeks later ('Arianna or Germaine? Readers' views on woman's role in society today', *The Australian Women's Weekly*, November 6, 1974). *The Australian Women's Weekly*'s nearest competitor, *Woman's Day* followed its lead, publishing excerpts from *The Female Woman* over the course of three consecutive editions, also with front cover headlines in the first two cases ('The female woman', *Woman's Day*, October 21, 1974; 'The female woman (Part 2): The sexual woman', *Woman's Day*, October 28, 1974; 'The female woman (Part 3): The family woman', *Woman's Day*, November 4, 1974).

Once in Australia, Stassinopoulos began to receive attention not just in the women's magazines but in major newspapers. Along with her arrival in Sydney, her subsequent visits to Brisbane, Melbourne and Adelaide all prompted separate local press coverage ('The "female woman" takes on the Libbers', *The Courier-Mail*, November 19, 1974; 'Face to face and poles apart on women's lib', *The Age*, November 23, 1974; 'Women should "not feel guilt" in housewife role, *The Advertiser*, November 27, 1974). Numerous book reviews of *The Female Woman* also followed, at least two of which were by critics who had previously reviewed *The Female Eunuch* ('The feminist manifesto', *The Canberra Times*, January 8, 1972; 'A defence of the victors'; 'A dream of sisterhood', *The Advertiser*, April 24, 1971; 'One woman's view of Liberationists', *The Advertiser*, November 30, 1974). In addition, Stassinopoulos made a number of television and radio appearances, including on the ABC's program, Monday Conference, which generated further coverage in the print media ('Few women are supporting women's liberation', *The Australian*, November 19, 1974; 'Libbers want to be "imitation men"', *The Advertiser*, November 19, 1974; 'A manicured fist for women's lib', *The Australian*, November 23, 1974; 'The "female woman" takes on the Libbers').

While the Australian visit was part of a wider international tour, the extensive media coverage that accompanied it offers a particularly valuable case study through which to consider the implications of Stassinopoulos' book for popular understandings of Greer. The tendency to privilege Greer as not just one expression of feminism, but as *the* representative figure of feminism has been especially noticeable in Australia, both in relation to understandings of contemporary feminism and the feminist past (Dux and Simic 2008, 4; Henderson 2006, 149–153). This view of Greer as synonymous with women's liberation had first emerged in the context of her own visit to Australia in the summer of 1971–1972 to promote *The Female Eunuch*, though it also competed then with representations of Greer as different from – and, critically, more likeable than – other women's liberationists (Lilburn, Magarey, and Sheridan 2000, 344). As will become evident, Greer's earlier visit was more generally a significant factor in determining various dynamics of the media coverage during Stassinopoulos' tour.

The timing of Stassinopoulos' visit to Australia was also particularly significant. Australia was distinctive in this period in having undergone a rapid transformation following the election of a Labor Government in December 1972, after 23 years of conservative rule. Stassinopoulos' visit took place at a critical juncture, at a point when the feminist movement was gaining political momentum under the new government and just ahead of International Women's Year (IWY) in 1975 (Curthoys 1992, 436; Lake 1999, 258–259), but also at a time when the first signs of a more organised backlash against feminism were becoming apparent, driven in large part by a fear that feminists had succeeded in 'capturing the policy-making processes of Australian politics' (Webley 1983, 8). By 1974, several Christian-based, pro-family groups had formed, including the Australian Festival of Light and the Family Action Movement.[9] Various attempts at abortion law reform in particular had spurred organised opposition in several states and territories, with the formation of the first right to life associations from 1972, while proposed changes to family law were being vigorously opposed at the time of Stassinipoulos' visit, with some success (*The Australian*, November 30, 1974).

To what extent Stassinopoulos' visit can be directly linked to local anti-feminist groups is unclear. On the one hand, it does not appear that Stassinopoulos had any direct contact with these groups during her visit.[10] Her more liberal views on sexual politics may have contributed to this lack of engagement; that said, these differences did not prevent later organisations, such as Women Who Want to be Women, formed in 1979, from citing her work where it was convenient for them (Webley 1982, 137).[11] On the other hand, there are obvious parallels between Stassinopoulos' views and those articulated by the Women's Action Alliance (WAA), a new group formed in April 1975, just five months after her visit. Putting itself forward as the representative of Australian housewives, the WAA defended the right to 'choose' to stay at home and the value of the family and marriage, while also stating that it was 'firmly' committed to equal pay and remaining silent on the subject of abortion ('Mothers are VIPs', *The Australian Women's Weekly*, June 18, 1975). Given the timing, it is possible that her visit contributed to the impetus behind its establishment; certainly, members of the group were familiar with her book.[12] Whereas Stassinopoulos' visit can only tentatively be linked with local backlash groups, its importance in shaping popular discourse around feminism is much more apparent from the media coverage Stassinopoulos was able to generate. Arguably her key contribution to the emergence of backlash politics in Australia was to bring unprecedented publicity to the anti-feminist cause via this media presence. Her use of Greer was one of the main determinants of her capacity to generate this media interest.

Capitalising on Greer's celebrity: media coverage of the Stassinopoulos/Greer rivalry

Stassinopoulos' framing of *The Female Woman* as a response to *The Female Eunuch* was undoubtedly one of the key factors in attracting media coverage of her 1974 tour. Much of the publicity in the lead up to and during the tour hinged on the notion that Stassinopoulos was Greer's major adversary. Indeed, while there were some exceptions, media stories that did not mention Greer in connection with Stassinopoulos were very much in the minority. Of the news stories examined here, only three did not refer to Greer and all were short news stories ('Libbers want to be "imitation men"'; '"Libbers" opponent speaks up', *The Canberra Times*, November 19, 1974; 'Few women are supporting women's liberation'). It was clear that one of the reasons why Stassinopoulos was considered to be newsworthy was because of Greer's own celebrity.

The most sustained use of the Stassinopoulos/Greer opposition as a framing device can be found in *The Australian Women's Weekly*'s profile piece on Stassinopoulos in the lead up to her visit. Entitled 'Arianna's gunning for you, Germaine', it described Stassinopoulos as Greer's 'strongest critic' and the book as a 'direct attack' on *The Female Eunuch*. The article itself opened with a direct quote from Stassinopoulos, which summed up many of her major criticisms of Greer, including that she was 'out of touch', 'elitist' and, crucially, that she 'projects from her own personal problems: her unhappy childhood, unhappy marriage, and unhappy choice of men'. The article went on to note the refusal of Greer to debate Stassinopoulos and concluded with a comparison of their publication records. Importantly, no other individual feminists were mentioned in the article, although it did distinguish Greer from the 'lesbians' and the 'lunatic fringe' of the movement. Continuing the theme of the article itself, a full page of letters appeared in a subsequent edition of the magazine under the banner, 'Arianna or Germaine?'. Three of the responses to Stassinopoulos specifically referenced Greer, suggesting that the representation of the two women as rivals had resonated with the magazine's readers, although, as I will show, even the two letters that were favourable to Stassinopoulos did not necessarily reject Greer outright, complicating the Stassinopoulos/Greer opposition in important ways.

While the sustained use of the Stassinopoulos/Greer comparison throughout *The Australian Women's Weekly* article and in the reader responses was especially striking, references to the two women as rivals were by no means uncommon. The front-page story in *The Sydney Morning Herald* announcing Stassinopoulos' arrival in Australia was headlined 'Women's lib's worst friend: a hefty swipe at Germaine', a claim that was repeated in the story and in a modified version that appeared in *The Courier-Mail* three days later ('The "female woman" takes on the Libbers'). Elsewhere Stassinopoulos was referred to as 'Britain's best known anti-Greerite', 'Britain's answer to Germaine Greer' and Greer's 'arch enemy' ('Perspective', *The Australian*, November 11, 1974; 'Perspective', *The Australian*, November 12, 1974; 'Women's Lib all Greek to her'; 'Sylvia's woman to women', *Sunday Mail*, November 24, 1974). A more subtle comparison between the two was made in an article in *The Age* via a reference to Stassinopoulos as the 'high priestess of femininity' ('Women's Lib all Greek to her'), evoking earlier descriptions of Greer as the 'high priestess' of women's liberation ('Beast just wants to survive in a world without any eunuchs', *The Age*, January 21, 1972; Spongberg 1993, 407).

As in *The Australian Women's Weekly* article, much was also made of the fact that Greer had refused to appear against Stassinopoulos in debates or to meet her. This claim re-emerged in *The Sydney Morning Herald*'s article on Stassinopoulos' arrival; it reported that, when asked by a reporter whether the two had met each other, Stassinopoulos had replied 'sweetly' she would 'love' to do so but that Greer had refused to debate her on three occasions ('Women's lib's worst friend: a hefty swipe at Germaine'). This was reproduced the following day in a longer profile piece on Stassinopoulos in *The Sun-Herald* and subsequently appeared in multiple newspapers surveyed for this article ('Arianna is no friend of women's lib ...', *The Sun-Herald*, November 17, 1974; 'Women's Lib all Greek to her'; 'Enter the female woman who is oh, so anti-lib'). Furthermore, a related charge of censorship appeared in some of these later articles. Stassinopoulos claimed that Greer had personally tried to dissuade the editor of *The London Observer* from serialising *The Female Woman* ('Arianna is no friend of women's lib ... '). More generally, she alleged that she had been the subject of censorship by the media in England and America ('Enter the female woman who is oh, so anti-lib'). Importantly, Greer was presented here as an unfair player who was not even willing to defend her views. Stassinopoulos, on the other hand, was presented as a charismatic figure who was a worthy rival of Greer's.

As well as the explicit references to Stassinopoulos as an opponent of Greer, this positioning of the two women as personal adversaries was sustained in a more general sense through an emphasis on Stassinopoulos' youth, beauty and intellect. Stassinopoulos was presented as a glamorous figure, who dressed in 'elegant French silk' and wore 'ruby nailpolish' ('Enter the female woman who is oh, so anti-lib'; 'The "female woman" takes on the Libbers'), but who also had 'impeccable intellectual credentials' ('Arianna's gunning for you, Germaine'; 'The female woman', *The Sydney Morning Herald*, November 28, 1974). In particular, her Cambridge degree and formidable debating skills were repeatedly emphasised ('Face to face and poles apart on women's lib'; 'Sylvia's woman to women'). Photographs of Stassinopoulos contributed to this representation of Stassinopoulos as both feminine and intellectual. Images of a smiling and confident Stassinopoulos accompanied many of the early stories on Stassinopoulos; this is how she appeared, for example, in *The Australian Women's Weekly* profile and in stories after her initial press conference. However, she was also photographed in earnest conversation ('Arianna is no friend of women's lib ... ') and, sometimes, in serious debating mode ('Face to face ... Women's Lib. and the "Female Woman"'). Regardless, Stassinopoulos was always well-dressed, made up and poised; her femininity remained uncompromised.

Stassinopoulos' presentation of herself as feminine and intellectual was critical in positioning her as an effective counter-figure to Greer. Though Greer was often described as attractive and played on her heterosexual appeal to bolster her mainstream appeal, including among women (Le Masurier 2007a, 210–211; Spongberg 1993; Wallace 1997, 245), she was not 'pretty' in a conventional sense like Stassinopoulos. Moreover, like other women's liberationists, Greer presented a searing critique of traditional femininity in *The Female Eunuch*. This aspect of their rivalry was generally only implicit, but on at least one occasion Stassinopoulos was herself invited to comment on Greer's appearance, conceding to a *Sydney Morning Herald* reporter that Greer 'is a very attractive woman ... sometimes' ('Arianna is no friend of women's lib ... '). Stassinopoulos made it clear she represented a different mode of womanhood to Greer: that of the 'female woman'.

One of the reasons that Stassinopoulos' rivalry with Greer captivated the media was the sheer thrill of seeing Greer attacked by another woman in such a public way. The Australian media attributed some authority to Stassinopoulos' views simply on the basis that *The Female Woman* was an anti-women's liberation text written by a woman, underlining the importance of women's involvement in anti-feminist organisations in the 1970s in lending legitimacy to the backlash as representing the interests of women (Power and Bacchetta 2002; Rowland 1984; Webley 1982, 1983). Stassinopoulos was not alone by any means in occupying this position; indeed, during Greer's own visit in the summer of 1971–1972, some of the most sensational media coverage had stemmed from public criticism by other women (Lilburn, Magarey, and Sheridan 2000, 342). Nonetheless there was still some sense of novelty to this fact, particularly in the Australian context, where women's involvement was yet to become a prominent feature of the organised backlash. Moreover, this novelty was heightened by the fact that, unlike the female commentators who had attacked Greer during her own visit, notably in the form of three contentious book reviews (Lilburn, Magarey, and Sheridan 2000, 341–343), Stassinopoulos fit the very demographic that seemed to be women's liberation's key constituency.

One effect of the media focus on the rivalry between Stassinopoulos and Greer was to perpetuate the idea that Greer was synonymous with women's liberation. Greer was overwhelmingly the most cited feminist – and typically the only feminist cited – in relation to Stassiniopoulos in the lead up to and during the Australian tour; a few reports also referred to Millett ('Face to face … Women's Lib. and the "Female Woman"'; 'The "female woman" takes on the Libbers'; 'Women's Lib claws are at the ready'; 'Women's Lib's worst friend: a hefty swipe at Germaine') and one referred to Gloria Steinem ('Arianna is no friend of women's lib … '), but they were never given the same kind of prominence as Greer. In keeping with the overriding message of Stassinopoulos' own book, this focus on Greer positioned her unquestionably as the figurehead of women's liberation, failing to acknowledge debates around Greer's capacity to represent the movement. This view was further reinforced by aspects of the media coverage of feminist reactions to Stassinopoulos' visit, but also complicated in various ways that allowed for a more complex discussion around the feminist politics of leadership and representation.

Moving beyond Greer?: Media coverage of feminist reactions to Stassinopoulos

While Stassinopoulos' strategic use of Greer's celebrity to publicise her text was a key factor in making her book tour newsworthy, it was also the broader context of the feminist movement's growing political momentum and the emerging backlash against it that contributed significantly to making her visit a major event. In this climate of contest, it was not just Stassinopoulos' attacks on Greer that captivated the media, but also local feminist responses to her visit. Indeed, in the absence of Greer herself to debate Stassinopoulos (and her reported failure to do so in Britain), local feminists became a focus of media attention during the Australian visit. As noted earlier, *Cleo*'s initial publication of excerpts from *The Female Woman* prompted a sharp reply from women's liberation member Judy Gemmel. This set the pattern for coverage during the tour, in which women's liberation's reactions were central to the drama of Stassinopoulos' visit. During and in the immediate aftermath of the visit, feminist comment was directly invited by media outlets; for example, well-known activist Anne Summers, who had previously written a review of Greer's *The Female Eunuch* for *The Advertiser*, followed up with review of *The Female Woman*, in late November ('One woman's view of Liberationists').[13] In addition, various encounters between Stassinopoulos and Australian activists also made the news. Multiple media outlets reported on the decision of Sydney women's liberation to boycott Stassinopoulos' appearance on the Monday Conference. In addition, *The Courier-Mail* featured a half-page report on a debate between Stassinopoulos and Barbara Wertheim, the research and planning officer of the Women's Community Aid Association, formed by women's liberationists in Brisbane in 1973 ('Face to face … Women's Lib. and the "Female Woman"'; Henderson and Reid 2004), while

Melbourne's *The Age* featured a conversation between Stassinopoulos and Eve Mahlab, a business woman and member of the Women's Electoral Lobby, a reform-oriented group that had formed in 1972 out of women's liberation ('Face to face and poles apart on women's lib'; Sawer 2008).

One of the effects of this reporting was to extend the spectacle of the Greer/Stassinopoulos opposition to local activists. This was especially evident in media reporting on the decision of Sydney women's liberation to boycott the ABC's Monday Conference. The program followed a standard format in which the host, Robert Moore, interviewed the guest speaker in front of a live audience, with participation considered to be a key feature. *The Australian*'s John Lapsley was the first to pick up on the stand-off, reporting on 11 November in his column, 'Perspective', that Sydney women's liberation had refused to participate in the program on the basis that Stassinopoulos was 'ill-researched and trivial' and that attending was a 'total waste of time'. He followed up the next day, reporting that the ABC had since 'mustered 14 souls prepared to stand and do battle for Women's Lib'; they were, he observed, perhaps more accurately described as 'scabs' breaking rank from the 'organised' section of the movement. Importantly, the major lure of the story of Sydney women's liberation's boycott of Stassinopoulos was not just the conflict between Stassinopoulos and women's liberation but the emerging divisions among feminists themselves. At the same time, his earlier commentary reproduced Stassinopoulos' view of Greer as synonymous with women's liberation: the contest was no longer simply between Stassinopoulos and Greer, but between Stassinopoulos and 'a host of Greerites' ('Perspective', November 6, 1974). Greer and women's liberation were assumed to be one and the same.

However, other media coverage of feminist responses to Stassinopoulos' visit provided some space to complicate this view of Greer and women's liberation as synonymous. Feminist criticisms of Stassinopoulos for misrepresenting women's liberation as a uniform movement were a recurrent theme in media coverage. For instance, Summers' review of *The Female Woman* in *The Advertiser* described Stassinopoulos as being 'guilty of a profound ignorance of ideas and practice' in relation to the feminist movement and specifically located this problem in Stassinopoulos' reliance on a few key works. Stassinopoulos 'thinks WLM consists only of Kate Millett, Germaine Greer and a smattering of other women who have managed to achieve publication', she wrote ('One woman's view of Liberationists'). In a similar vein, Wertheim objected that the book was 'far too naïve and simplistic' in its depiction of women's liberation, which comprised a 'vast number of organisations' ('Face to face ... Women's Lib. and the "Female Woman"').

More generally, feminist responses aimed to create distance between Greer and women's liberation. Mahlab emphasised that being a 'liberated woman' did not mean being bound by 'the doctrine of Germaine Greer' as Stassinopoulos claimed ('Face to face and poles apart on women's lib'), while the one openly feminist respondent to the *The Australian Women's Weekly*'s article on Stassinopoulos emphasised that women's liberation was not for women like Greer who would succeed 'no matter what the odds' but rather for 'the poor, the underprivileged, the emotionally and intellectually deprived' ('Arianna or Germaine?'). Local feminists' willingness to debate Stassinopoulos was also contrasted with Greer's refusal to do so; *The Courier-Mail* made a particular point of this in order to talk up the significance of the Brisbane debate between Wertheim and

Stassinopoulos, almost proudly asserting that Stassinopoulos 'had found no "takers" till she came to Brisbane' ('Face to face ... Women's Lib. and the "Female Woman"').

In addition to complicating Stassinopoulos' conflation of Greer and women's liberation, media coverage of feminist responses to Stassinopoulos' visit also provided an opportunity to extend discussion about what exactly Greer and women's liberation more generally stood for. In their exchanges with Stassinopoulos, her local opponents sought to raise substantive issues around family, sexuality, work and women's bodies and offer an alternative perspective to that presented by Stassinopoulos. In *The Courier-Mail*, Wertheim and Stassinopoulos debated women's role in raising children and the politics of personal relationships. Wertheim, the mother of six children, countered Stassinopoulos' claims that feminism was anti-mother by emphasising that women's liberation recognised the 'great joy' in raising children, but also the 'strains and stresses' on parents within the nuclear family structure ('Face to face ... Women's Lib. and the "Female Woman"'). In *The Age*, Mahlab took Stassinopoulos up on her views on work, including the question of the housewife, countering the latter's claim that women's liberation created anxiety for women about staying home by pointing to the wider social conditions that contributed to this feeling, including the increasing numbers of women in the workforce ('Face to face and poles apart on women's lib'). As such, Stassinopoulos' views did not go uncontested in these forums.

Ultimately, the degree of attention given to local activists' responses to Stassinopoulos was in itself significant in validating feminist perspectives on these issues. The overall impression created by this coverage was that Stassinopoulos' position was controversial and that she could not be given a platform without also presenting an opposing view. What was evident here was the media's tacit recognition that feminism had gained wide popular appeal and that at least some of their readers expected to see Stassinopoulos' views challenged. Crucially, the very fact the local feminist responses to Stassinopoulos were a focus of the media coverage represented a form of acknowledgement that women's liberation consisted of more than Greer. At the same time, Greer's own popular appeal was also important in moderating the extent to which Stassinopoulos was able to gain traction and advance her claim to represent the 'average' woman, the final aspect of the media coverage of the Australian tour to be considered here.

Competing for the 'average' woman

'Millions of words have been written, and shouted, by the leaders of women's liberation ... Now a beautiful Greek-born girl with an impressive academic background has spoken up, loudly and clearly, for the average woman – the REAL woman'. *Woman's Day*'s introduction to their first excerpt from *The Female Woman* could not have endorsed Stassinopoulos in stronger terms ('The female woman'). Complemented by a front cover headline that declared the book to be the 'most challenging book yet ... about YOU', the magazine made it clear that Stassinopoulos was an advocate for the 'average' woman. Much of the general news coverage of the visit likewise picked up on Stassinopoulos' claim to represent the 'average' woman, in contrast to Greer and women's liberation who represented a select 'elite'. Although reported in more neutral terms, this view was largely allowed to go uncontested, as reflected in headlines such as *The Australian*'s 'Few women are supporting women's liberation'.

Stassinopoulos' capacity to present herself as the representative of 'ordinary' women depended in part on her appeal to domesticity. It was Stassinopoulos' defence of the housewife that gained the most traction in the media coverage leading up to and during her visit. Media reports repeatedly emphasised that Stassinopoulos' objective was to defend the right of women to 'choose' to be mothers and wives and *The Advertiser* specifically picked up on this theme in its headline, 'Women should "not feel guilt" in housewife role'. Stassinopoulos herself played up her success in reaching this group, telling a reporter from *The Age* that she had received 'a large bouquet ... sent by a housewife with a card reading: "for all the things you have done for the women at home"' ('Face to face and poles apart on women's lib'). Meanwhile, with the exception of feminists such as Mahlab, Stassinopoulos' charge that women's liberation treated housewives as 'inferior' was repeated with little challenge.

Stassinopoulos was by no means alone in making the case that housewives had been alienated by women's liberation and some feminist historians have since offered critical accounts of the movement on this basis. Australian historian Lesley Johnson, for example, has argued that the housewife was constructed as an 'other' in second-wave feminist writings; as 'one who needs to be rescued, liberated or left behind' (Johnson 2000, 237). Crucially this was a point on which Greer had herself been repeatedly condemned, including during her 1971–1972 visit, which saw a number of prominent attacks on her as an 'elitist' who was out of touch with 'ordinary' women, a charge that was closely tied to her critique of domesticity (Lilburn, Magarey, and Sheridan 2000, 342). Stassinopoulos' claim to speak for housewives offered a clear continuation of this line of critique.

Yet, it is also clear that Stassinopoulos' claim to represent the 'average' woman depended on more than positioning herself as the defender of housewives. It was also important for Stassinopoulos to combine this message with her assertion that she was in favour of 'equality' and thus acknowledge certain feminist goals. Stassinopoulos' blend of individualism and social conservatism was foregrounded in *The Australian*'s article announcing her arrival, which noted that she was for 'the family, ... children ... marriage .... strong social values and innate differences between the sexes' but 'also believes in a tolerant society, equal pay, equal opportunity, equal rights ... abortion and homosexual law reform' ('Enter the female woman who is oh, so anti-lib'). It was also a consistent theme in coverage in women's magazines. *Woman's Day* stated that Stassinopoulos was sympathetic to those women who 'are distressed by the unfeminine image the leaders of women's lib are presenting' but 'believe in equal rights and equal pay' ('The female woman'). *The Australian Women's Weekly* described her as 'a champion of women' and drew attention to her support for legislative change. Reader responses provide further evidence that this message was central to Stassinopoulos' appeal, with various women framing their support for Stassinopoulos in terms of their belief in 'equal opportunity' and 'equal choice' ('Arianna or Germaine?').

Women's magazines' endorsement of Stassinopoulos on the basis that she was still in favour of 'equality' was indicative of the impact that feminism had already had on these spaces. While considerably more conservative than *Cleo*, both *The Australian Women's Weekly* and *Woman's Day* had featured articles on the women's liberation movement and related subjects, such as the housework debate. Women's liberation was topical and 'could not be ignored' by these magazines, especially *The Australian Women's Weekly*, which had a strong news orientation (Sherian 2001, 153). Importantly, Greer had herself received sympathetic coverage in the two magazines, albeit in somewhat equivocal terms. In the lead up to and during Greer's 1971–1972 tour, articles in the two magazines had variously described Greer as 'brilliant', 'warmhearted', 'witty' and 'fun', and had also made sure to emphasise her heterosexuality ('What women's liberation means to Germaine Greer', Woman's Day, December 27, 1971; 'Germaine Greer talks', The Australian Women's Weekly, November 24, 1971; 'The liberating of Germaine Greer', Australian Women's Weekly, February 2, 1972). Greer's personal life had also been a focus of coverage and, in contrast to Stassinopoulos' attempts to pathologise Greer, this coverage had served to humanise her; she was 'honest and uninhibited', The Australian Women's Weekly's reporter, Kay Keavney, concluded ('The liberating of Germaine Greer'). Through this sympathetic coverage, the two magazines had helped to validate Greer in the eyes of their readers.

In turn, Greer's own popularity proved to be a key factor in mediating Stassinopoulos' appeal. Reader responses to The Australian Women's Weekly article show that even some of those who endorsed Stassinopoulos acknowledged Greer specifically as having had a positive impact. Mrs G. M. of Moe, Victoria, explained that, like Stassinopoulos, she had been 'sickened' by most of Greer's views, yet she still noted that Greer had 'succeeded in getting men to re-appraise and reappreciate [sic]' women. Meanwhile C. F. Little, of Swan Reach, Victoria, offered a reinterpretation of Stassinopoulos not as a rival but a successor to Greer. When Greer had 'started Women's Liberation', a 'better deal for women, everywhere, was long overdue', she wrote. She understood Stassinopoulos' 'softer, more moderate outlook' to 'follow on the good work' of Greer but implored that other readers 'not forget her predecessor who paved the way for a softer approach' ('Arianna or Germaine?'). One can also see this moderating effect elsewhere in the media coverage of Stassinopoulos' visit, including when she was herself forced to concede that Greer was 'attractive' and 'a very bright and a very articulate person' ('Arianna is no friend of women's lib … '; 'Women's Lib all Greek to her').

Herein lay one of the ironies of Stassinopoulos' attempts to capitalise on Greer's celebrity for the purposes of backlash politics and her own career. In positioning herself as an opponent to Greer, Stassinopoulos was attacking a figure who was ultimately still popular with some of those in her target audience or, at the very least, who was understood to have made a positive contribution to women's lives. Stassinopoulos' invoking of Greer in order to advance her claim to represent the 'average' woman was thus only a partially successful strategy and, in some cases, was decidedly risky. Where Stassinopoulos claimed that Greer was irrelevant to 'ordinary' women, her very dependence on Greer as a cultural symbol of women's liberation was a telling sign of Greer's lasting influence and kept Greer at the forefront of public debate about the merits of feminism in this period.

Conclusion

Stassinopoulos' The Female Woman depended in large part on The Female Eunuch and the reputation of Greer herself in order to publicise its anti-feminist message. To the extent that this attempt to capitalise on Greer's own celebrity served to attract media interest in Stassinopoulos, this appeal to Greer as cultural symbol of women's liberation proved to be a successful strategy. Herself a highly charismatic figure, Stassinopoulos gained unprecedented media coverage for the anti-feminist cause during the lead up to and during her visit to

Australia and it is clear that her rivalry with Greer was a crucial factor in securing this attention. It also provided a powerful template for local anti-feminist activists, who would continue to attack Greer in the years to come.[14] The media storm that surrounded Stassinopoulos' under-examined visit to Australia is thus a reminder of the importance of paying closer attention to the early emergence of backlash politics in Australia, including the role of international figures in shaping local anti-feminist discourses. While there has been some work on anti-feminist groups in Australia, a full account of the backlash has yet to be produced and may help to provide a clearer account of Stassinopoulos' own impact.

On the other hand, to view the media attention given to Stassinopoulos simply as a victory for backlash politics would be short-sighted. While her visit to Australia was clearly a vehicle for the promotion of anti-feminist sentiment, this was by no means its only outcome. As this article has demonstrated, Stassinopoulos' visit was also a validating moment for feminism and for Greer more specifically. To begin with, Stassinopoulos' own appeal depended on her willingness to accommodate certain feminist goals; this made it possible for some to reinterpret Stassinopoulos as a 'successor' to Greer rather than opponent. In addition, extensive media coverage of feminist responses to Stassinopoulos' tour, while sometimes sensationalised and reduced to a form of spectacle, made it clear that Stassinopoulos' views were contentious and also served to complicate various claims Stassinopoulos made about women's liberation itself, including her tendency to equate Greer with women's liberation as a whole. Thus, while one effect of the book and the publicity around it was to perpetuate a view of Greer as synonymous with women's liberation, it also offered an opportunity to extend discussions of the feminist politics of leadership and representation into the public arena.

Ultimately, the tour represented a test not just of Stassinopoulos' capacity to gain traction in Australia, but a test of Greer's own appeal. In this respect, Stassinopoulos' use of Greer in order to attack women's liberation more generally proved to be a risky strategy. Greer's own popularity proved to be a key factor in mediating against Stassinopoulos' appeal and particularly her capacity to advance her claim to represent the 'average' woman. Though Stassinopoulos was given a prominent platform in Australia to spruik her anti-feminist message, we should be careful not to overstate the success of her tour. There was ample evidence that feminism retained popular appeal, despite the emerging signs of backlash. Greer's celebrity – the very quality that Stassinopoulos sought to exploit for her own benefit – was key here in serving as a powerful countervailing force to Stassinopoulos' anti-feminist attack.

Notes

1. It was preceded by American writer Decter's *The Liberated Woman and Other Americans* (1971) and *The New Chastity and Other Arguments against Women's Liberation* (1972). Marabel Morgan's *The Total Woman* (1973), another key backlash text, was published the same year as Stassinopoulos' book.
2. Unlike other key figures, such as Decter and Morgan, Stassinopoulos is not included in sections on the backlash against feminism in widely cited works such as Bouchier's *The Feminist Challenge: The Movement for Women's Liberation in Britain and the United States* (1983) and Rosen's *The World Split Open* (2006). Stassinoulos' 1974 tour is not mentioned in the major book-length accounts of the Australian movement (Kaplan 1996; Lake 1999; Sawer 1990, 2008). Media

scholar Le Masurier (2007b, 201) provides a brief analysis of Stassinopoulos' work in relation to *Cleo*'s decision to publish the excerpt from Stassinopoulos' book.
3. The same newspapers were used by Lilburn, Magarey, and Sheridan (2000) in their study of Greer's book tour in 1971–1972, providing a useful comparative model on assessing national coverage.
4. By way of comparison, Kate Millet receives 16 page mentions, Shulamith Firestone five, Simone De Beauvoir two, Betty Friedan one, and Eva Figes one.
5. *The Female Eunuch* was discussed at women's liberation meetings and was regularly recommended in early reading lists. As has previously been noted, it was reviewed by Adelaide activist Anne Summers in *The Advertiser* (April 24, 1971). In addition, a little-known review by Sydney women's liberationist Camille Guy (1971) appeared in the country's first feminist newspaper, *Mejane*, published in March 1971.
6. For example, women's liberationists attended Greer's address at the National Press Club Luncheon in Canberra in January 1972, and organised a protest in Sydney after the ABC refused to broadcast footage of Greer speaking as part of a debate on abortion held at Sydney Town Hall in March 1972. Both events were reported on in *Mejane* (No author 1972; Norie 1972).
7. The first version of this essay was published in the women's liberation journal, *The Second Wave*, in 1972.
8. Gemmel also published a review of *The Female Woman* in the Melbourne women's liberation journal, *Vashti's Voice* (Gemmel 1974–1975).
9. The Australian Festival of Light (FoL) was modelled on the British organisation of the same name. It was initially formed in Adelaide in 1972, with state committees subsequently set up in Melbourne and Sydney in 1973. Mary Whitehouse was invited to Australia to launch the FoL in October 1973 (Gibson 2009, 55; Nile 2001, 90). A related political party, the Family Action Movement, was formed in 1974 and fielded three candidates, Rev. Fred Nile, Frieda Brown and Ken Harrison, in the federal election held on 18 May 1974, with endorsement from FoL (*Festival of Light News Bulletin*, May, 1974).
10. Unlike her oppositional encounters with local feminists, no contact between Stassinopoulos and conservative organisations were reported in the media. In addition, her visit to Australia did not register in the internal publicity of the Festival of Light at the time and is not mentioned in the autobiography of one of its key members, Rev. Fred Nile, who was then New South Wales state director.
11. Women Who Want to Be Women (WWWW) was formed by a group of dissidents within the WAA in 1979 as a result of the organisation's failure to take a clear stance against abortion. It quickly superseded the WAA to become the preeminent anti-feminist group in Australia (Webley 1982, 1983). WWWW included *The Female Woman* in its booklist prepared as part of a campaign to have anti-feminist literature included in university libraries and courses (Webley 1982, 137).
12. For example, *The Female Woman* featured in an early list of reading material circulated within the organisation (*Women's Action Alliance Newsletter*, October, 1975).
13. In addition, sympathetic journalist Yvonne Preston published a review of *The Female Woman* in *The National Times*, a weekly current affairs newspaper ('For the Woman Who Has Everything, Liberation is Dangerous Nonsense', *National Times*, December 2–7, 1974).
14. Like Stassinopoulos, for example, the WAA made Greer one of their early targets, objecting to her having 'represented' Australian women at an IWY symposium held at the United Nations in New York in March 1975 ('Mothers are VIPs') and to a controversial grant of $100,000 made to her by the IWY National Advisory Committee to produce a documentary on human reproduction (*Women's Action Alliance Newsletter*, October, 1975; Grieve 1987, 72–73).

Acknowledgements

The author wishes to thank Dr Zora Simic for her feedback on an earlier version of this article, the two anonymous reviewers for their helpful suggestions, and the journal editors for their assistance and mentoring throughout the process of writing this article. Isobelle Barrett Meyering developed this article as a 2015 participant in the AFS Mentoring Program for New Academic Writers.

Disclosure statement

No potential conflict of interest was reported by the author.

References

Bouchier, David. 1983. *The Feminist Challenge: The Movement for Women's Liberation in Britain and the United States*. London: Macmillan Press.

Bradley, Patricia. 2003. *Mass Media and the Shaping of American Feminism, 1963–1975*. Jackson: University Press of Mississippi.

Curthoys, Ann. 1992. "Doing It for Themselves: The Women's Movement since 1970." In *Gender Relations in Australia: Domination and Negotiation*, edited by Kay Saunders and Raymond Evans, 425–447. Sydney: Harcourt Brace Jovanovich.

Decter, Midge. 1971. *The Liberated Woman and Other Americans*. New York: Coward, McCann & Geoghegan.

Decter, Midge. 1972. *The New Chastity and Other Arguments against Women's Liberation*. New York: Coward, McCann & Geoghegan.

Dux, Monica, and Zora Simic. 2008. *The Great Feminist Denial*. Melbourne: Melbourne University Press.

Faludi, Susan. 1992. *Backlash: The Undeclared War on Women*. London: Vintage.

Freeman, Jo. 1972–1973. "The Tyranny of Structurelessness." *Berkeley Journal of Sociology* 17: 151–164.

Gemmel, Judy. 1974–1975. "The Female Woman." *Vashti's Voice* 9: 14.

Gibson, Sally E. 2009. "Creating Controversy: Sex Education and the Christian Right in South Australia." PhD diss., University of Adelaide.

Greer, Germaine. 1970. *The Female Eunuch*. London: MacGibbon & Kee.

Grieve, Anna. 1987. "Big Mother, Little Sister: The Women's Film Fund." In *Don't Shoot Darling! Women's Independent Filmmaking in Australia*, 69–83. Richmond: Greenhouse Publications.

Guy, Camille. 1971. "The Female Eunuch." *Mejane* 1 (1): 12.

Henderson, Margaret. 2006. *Marking Feminist Times: Remembering the Longest Revolution in Australia*. Bern: Peter Lang.

Henderson, Margaret, and Margaret Reid. 2004. ""It's Not That Bloody Far from Sydney": Notes Towards a Semiotic History of the Brisbane Women's Movement, 1973–1983." *Australian Feminist Studies* 19 (44): 159–168.

Johnson, Lesley. 2000. "'Revolutions Are Not Made by Down-Trodden Housewives.' Feminism and the Housewife." *Australian Feminist Studies* 15 (32): 237–248.

Kaplan, Gisela. 1996. *The Meagre Harvest: The Australian Women's Movement 1950s-1990s*. St Leonards: Allen & Unwin.

Lake, Marilyn. 1999. *Getting Equal: The History of Australian Feminism*. Sydney: Allen and Unwin.

Le Masurier, M. J. 2007a. "Fair Go: Cleo Magazine as Popular Feminism in 1970s Australia." PhD diss., University of Sydney.

Le Masurier, Megan. 2007b. "My Other, My Self." *Australian Feminist Studies* 22 (53): 191–211.

Lilburn, Sandra, Susan Magarey, and Susan Sheridan. 2000. "Celebrity Feminism as Synthesis: Germaine Greer, the Female Eunuch and the Australian Print Media." *Continuum: Journal of Media & Cultural Studies* 14 (3): 335–348.

Morgan, Marabel. 1973. *The Total Woman*. Old Tappan, NJ: F H Revell.

Nile, Fred. 2001. *Fred Nile: An Autobiography*. Sydney: Strand Publishing.

No author. 1972. "Vive Germaine." *Mejane* 1 (6): 3.

Norie. 1972. "Duckmanton Quacks in Fright." *Mejane* 1 (7): 4.

Power, Margaret, and Paola Bacchetta. 2002. "Introduction." In *Right-Wing Women: From Conservatives to Extremists around the World*, 1–18. New York: Routledge.

Rosen, Ruth. 2006. *The World Split Open: How the Modern Women's Movement Changed America*. Revised ed. New York: Penguin Books.

Rowland, Robyn, ed. 1984. *Women Who Do and Women Who Don't Join the Women's Movement*. London: Routledge & Kegan Paul.

Sawer, Marian. 2008. *Making Women Count: A History of the Women's Electoral Lobby in Australia*. Sydney: UNSW Press.

Sherian, Susan. 2001. *Who Was that Woman?: The Australian Women's Weekly in the Postwar Years*. Sydney: UNSW Press.

Solanas, Valerie. 1968. *SCUM Manifesto*. New York: Olympia Press.

Spongberg, Mary. 1993. "If She's So Great, How Come So Many Pigs Dig Her? Germaine Greer and the Malestream Press." *Women's History Review* 2 (3): 407–419.

Stassinopoulos, Arianna. 1973. *The Female Woman*. London: Davis-Poynter.

Stassinopoulos, Arianna. 1974. *The Female Woman*. Paperback edition. London: Fontana.

Taylor, Anthea. 2014. "Germaine Greer's Adaptable Celebrity." *Feminist Media Studies* 14 (5): 759–774.

Tyler, Imogen. 2007. "The Selfish Feminist: Public Images of Women's Liberation." *Australian Feminist Studies* 22 (53): 173–190.

Wallace, Christine. 1997. *Greer, Untamed Shrew*. Sydney: Pan Macmillan Australia.

Webley, Irene. 1982. "Women Who Want to Be Women." In *Australia and the New Right*, edited by Marian Sawer, 135–151. North Sydney: George Allen & Unwin.

Webley, Irene. 1983. "The New Right and Women Who Want to Be Women in Australian Politics in the 1980s." *Hecate* 9 (1–2): 7–34.

'If we had more like her we would no longer be the unheard majority': Germaine Greer's reception in the United States

Rebecca J. Sheehan

ABSTRACT
This article examines Germaine Greer's reception in the United States in 1971, the year that *The Female Eunuch* was first published there. Using hundreds of previously unexamined letters sent by television viewers after she hosted *The Dick Cavett Show*, the article explores the impact of Greer's media engagement and the overwhelmingly positive reception she received from this particular audience. The letters detail Greer's strength, intelligence, wit, and keen ability to communicate. They demonstrate that she educated many audience members about feminist issues including abortion and rape, and inspired pride in her female audience. The sympathetic portrait of Greer in these letters contrasts with the more polarised view of Greer in the print media responses to her: the mainstream print media portrayed and embraced Greer as its ideal non-threatening, attractive and heterosexual feminist, and American feminists dismissed her as an opportunist. Taken together, the unpublished audience letters and the print media sources provide a more complex portrait of Greer's reception and effectiveness. The letters speak for Greer and – now that they are available in Greer's carefully preserved personal archive – restore the voices of the ordinary people who helped to shape the history of feminism.

On 14 and 15 June 1971, after a successful guest appearance, Germaine Greer acted as the guest host of *The Dick Cavett Show* (*TDCS*), a late-night talk show on the American ABC television network. With panels of guests representing different ideological positions, Greer led a 90-minute conversation each night. On the first night, the topic was birth control and Greer focused on abortion. On the second night, Greer led a discussion about rape. Greer did not act as an impartial moderator. She took a clear pro-choice position on abortion, pointed out the hypocrisy she perceived in her guests' responses, and, during the discussion about rape, highlighted problematic notions of female sexual availability in a male-dominated culture. In these ways, she linked herself with liberal feminists who sought legislative reform of abortion laws, and with radical feminists who looked to revolutionise existing sex roles and the culture that dictated them. In response, Greer received 'more mail ... than any other guest in the program's history' (Daphne Productions 1971).

Greer may have been chosen to fill in for Dick Cavett while he was on holiday because the ABC network was implementing a new strategy to boost its ratings position from third ranked to first by increasing its sexual content (Levine 2007). In the preceding months, during the American publicity tour for her book, Greer had established a reputation for speaking frankly about sexual matters and for drawing large audiences. *The Female Eunuch*, published in the United States in 1971, in which she argued that women would be liberated through their sexual desire, was climbing the bestseller list. It had received glowing reviews from the mainstream American press who hailed its ideas as the most palatable of all the new wave of feminist literature. Greer had debated the celebrated novelist Norman Mailer at a sold out public event attended by prominent American writers, artists, intellectuals, activists, and media workers (Cohen 1988). She appeared in print, on radio and on television to discuss her book and women's issues. By June she had been identified as the feminist darling of the American media (Cantwell 1971). In that context, media players such as the ABC network must have seen Greer as a boon.

Greer's approach to the topics she discussed on *TDCS* demonstrates that she was not merely providing salacious content for a ratings hungry network or pushing an acceptable feminist agenda. Rather, she gave voice to critical aspects of women's liberation. Indeed, as she explained on many occasions, she believed it was her role to use the media to promote feminist issues as someone willing and able to do so. Yet, Greer has been criticised for courting and working with the mainstream media. At the time, when other radical feminists refused to engage with a mass media they viewed as hostile to their cause, Greer was vilified for personal profiteering and 'selling [out] feminism' (Dreifus [1971] 1973). Greer, it has since been argued, played into and became a pawn of the male-dominated media who used Greer and her arguments selectively to support their patriarchal and anti-feminist agendas (Spongberg 1993, 409). This kind of analysis has relied largely on published print sources about her, including those written by the mainstream media and her feminist contemporaries. These sources – in which the mainstream media favour Greer as a model of attractive and passionately heterosexual feminist womanhood, and feminists tend to criticise her as superficial and fake – give us a polarised and incomplete vision of Greer and a sense of second-wave feminism as an embattled movement with little public support.

A trove of previously unexamined television audience letters sent in response to Greer's turn as guest host of *TDCS* gives us a more complex picture of the impact of Greer's interaction with the media and its importance for promoting feminism. Hundreds of letters describe how in these two television appearances Greer gave voice to feminist issues in a way that no other feminist had done. The letters were sent mostly by women, although about a quarter were written by men, by viewers from their teens to viewers in their 80s, from all over the United States. Some writers identified as feminists but most did not. Although some – fewer than 20% – expressed horror at Greer and the topics she discussed as beneath respectability, the majority of the letters describe Greer as a woman unique and much-needed on television: strong, articulate, able to more than hold her own with men, and willing to discuss serious issues in depth, including birth control, abortion, and rape. Themes of gratitude and relief run through the letters; gratitude for Greer's willingness to do what she was doing in public and relief that she had the platform to do it.

These letters are in Greer's personal archive, which she began building from a young age, and which she sold to the University of Melbourne in 2013. While her archive has been institutionalised, its potential for producing knowledge has become possible in its new accessibility. The substantial reportage generated around the acquisition of the archive and its contents has underscored Greer's celebrity – reports have highlighted Greer's plans to use proceeds from the archive's sale for rainforest rehabilitation; listed her many famous correspondents, and buzzed over the unsent love letter she wrote to Martin Amis. Yet, rather than service any cult of celebrity around her, Greer has argued that the archive was always intended to serve history more broadly (Smith 2015). Claiming never to have thrown away 'a single piece of paper because each one was ... a witness' to an historical moment, Greer is proud that her archive's contents include many responses to her from 'ordinary people' 'expressing the way they feel' ("Germaine Greer speaks" 2013). In this, Greer demonstrates an activist approach to archiving of the kind that Eichhorn (2013, 6) argues restores 'not history itself but ... the ability to understand the condition of our everyday lives longitudinally'.

Indeed, the letters to *TDCS* give us rare insight into the thoughts of everyday Americans which are typically difficult to access or are simply absent from the historical record (Armstrong 2006).[1] Particularly when compared with published print responses to Greer, they show television's ability to communicate Greer at her most compelling, and its potential for broadcasting second-wave feminism. Via this television talk show, when Greer directed the conversation, the viewers appear to have received a greater sense of her charisma and ideas than print media could convey. Although the views in these letters cannot be read as representative of all Americans, they demonstrate a substantial and surprising level of support for Greer and the feminist issues she discussed. Such evidence contradicts accepted arguments about public resistance to feminism and what Engelhardt (2003, 60) has described as 'how threatening the politicized woman was in the public's mind'. The archival evidence also restores agency to an American public largely presumed to be passive recipients of negative ideas about feminism.

This article analyses these letters alongside feminist and mainstream media responses to Greer, and demonstrates that they add a significant dimension to our understanding of how Greer and second-wave feminism were interpreted and received. The letters show that Greer's willingness to work with the media was critical to the role she played in moving feminist issues into the American mainstream. There, she conveyed an inspiring model of complex and empowered womanhood, gave voice to issues of particular concern to women, and helped members of the American public to learn about – and embrace – aspects of women's liberation.

First published in Britain in 1970, Germaine Greer's *The Female Eunuch* argued that the patriarchal construction of women as passive beings had robbed women of their sexual energy and made them into eunuchs. By claiming their own active sexual pleasure, women would be liberated. The book became an instant bestseller there, and the British media's response created significant anticipation for the book's American publication. When it arrived in the United States in 1971, a *New York Times* headline introduced it as 'the best feminist book so far'. The reviewer, Christopher Lehmann-Haupt, expressed his wish that Greer's book had been the first of the current wave of feminist literature to be released and to receive the bulk of the attention – ahead, particularly, of American author

Kate Millett's *Sexual Politics* (Lehmann-Haupt 1971). Although both Millett and Greer called for a radical change to the existing gender order, he believed that Millett's work was too strident and masculine (Lehmann-Haupt 1970), whereas Greer's struck the right balance between fierce argument and femininity.

Most mainstream press articles about Greer in the United States portrayed Greer as a larger-than-life feminist. *Newsweek* reported that the women's liberation movement in Great Britain had lagged behind its American counterpart, but was ramping up,

> and rising out of today's version of this discontented distaff army, like an Amazon among the pygmies, is the awesome 6-foot figure of 32-year-old Germaine Greer, a dazzling combination of erudition, eccentricity and eroticism whose passionate treatise ... may well be women's lib's most realistic – and least anti-male – manifesto. ("The Female Eunuch" 1971, 48)

Greer's persona mattered as much, if not more, than her arguments in winning fans and converts: as *Newsweek* suggested, it was Greer herself who would make the book a bestseller in the United States. Another review in the *Seattle Post-Intelligencer* noted: 'Only a churl would choose patriarchal habit and privilege over this woman's intelligence, charm, and enviable independence of spirit' ("The Female Eunuch" 1971). Although most articles stressed that Greer rejected marriage, her charisma seemed to mitigate even that transgression. As Timothy Foote wrote in *Time*, 'One hesitates to call an opponent of marriage engaging, but Germaine Greer is certainly that' (Foote 1972). Widely described as beautiful, exotically Australian, a Shakespearean scholar at Cambridge, and passionately heterosexual, the American media positioned Greer in stark contrast to American feminists (Greenfield 1971; Weinraub 1971). In particular, they opposed her to Kate Millett, who had become the most famous feminist of 1970 and whose bisexuality had been used by the mainstream media to conflate feminism with lesbianism and discredit both (Hesford 2013). By repeatedly commenting on Greer's appearance, her pro-sex stance, and her attraction – and attractiveness – to men, these articles endorsed her as an ideal representative of women's liberation, a pro-male feminist who was a 'welcome change' from 'violent' homegrown feminists (Weinraub 1971; "Women's Liberation" 1971).

These reviews indicate that Greer's mainstream appeal was predicated on her heterosexual desirability rather than her ideas (Taylor 2014). A number of published feminist reviews contributed to a print media message that Greer had little else to offer. Sally Kempton, a member of New York Radical Feminists (founded by Shulamith Firestone and Anne Koedt, who were both critiqued by Greer in *TFE*), wondered whether the media were promoting what she described as, 'a [feminist] spokesman [sic] whose only qualification for the post was her ability to traffic with the enemy' (Kempton 1971). In the *Village Voice*, Jill Johnston called Greer 'an individually liberated woman whose background is such that very few women could interest her intellectually', and described her as a '"male identified woman" – the special woman who's made it in a man's world by learning the man's head and by a super combination of brains and body' (Johnston 1971).

That Greer was not a 'typical' woman was a common feminist criticism of her: it made the efficacy of her program – which seemed largely based on her own experience – questionable in terms of its application for ordinary people. Furthermore, she appeared to be overly critical of women's role in their own oppression. Writing in the *Harvard Educational Review*, Withorn (1971) expressed concern that Greer focused her anger on women rather than on oppressive systems. Withorn thought that Greer identified with men at the cost of other women; gave no credit to women for the agency they found within their limiting and limited social roles, and focused too much on individual transformation. Greer's focus on the individual was anathema to feminists such as Evelyn Reed, who believed that systemic revolution was critical to women's liberation. Greer failed, Reed argued, to offer any clear program to effect change, and was naïve to hope that it might happen organically (Reed 1971).

Claudia Dreifus was initially curious about Greer because, in her rise to fame, 'she was one of those truly self-made people. A cinderella [sic] who needed no prince' (Dreifus 1971). But later, in reviewing *The Female Eunuch* for *Nation*, Dreifus agreed with other feminist criticisms of it, calling the book 'shallow, anti-woman, regressive, three steps backward to the world of false sexual liberation from which so many young women have fled'. The title of Dreifus's article, 'The Selling of Feminism' (Dreifus [1971] 1973), summarised her perception that Greer was participating in the commodification of feminism. She argued that Greer did this through her heterosexuality and her appeal to women's sexual promiscuity. Dreifus's article was reprinted in a feminist paper and then a feminist anthology, which helped its circulation and citation and likely cemented the notion of Greer as a cynical opportunist who assisted the media in its perceived campaign against American feminism (Koedt and Firestone 1971; Koedt, Levine, and Rapone 1973).

Certainly, Greer benefited professionally and financially from the publicity she received. Yet, Greer was not unique; the paradox of empowerment via commodification was true of second-wave feminism in the 1970s more broadly. As Jill Johnston later commented, 'Our revolution ... was being funded and promoted by the male-owned and-run media' (Johnston 1998, 2–3). The symbiotic relationship between feminism and the media was problematic. As its responses to Germaine Greer demonstrated, the mainstream media played a role in constructing and feeding ideas of what feminism was about. It endorsed attractive, sexually available heterosexual feminists such as Greer and Gloria Steinem (Izzo 2002) over women it perceived to represent a radical change in sexual politics. At the same time, women's liberation benefited from media coverage, as increased visibility contributed to widespread consciousness-raising and the movement of feminist ideas into the mainstream (Cadden 1972; Dow 2014).

For Greer, this was precisely the reason to participate with the media. As she explained:

> The only reason ... I ever submit to the commercialization of Germaine Greer is to help women in the home, to raise the self-image of women, to spread the movement on the widest possible base. My aim is to demonstrate that everything could be otherwise, and joyously otherwise. ("Germaine Greer Tells" 1971)

In a *Playboy* interview, the only interview that a feminist gave to the magazine, Greer said that her role was to do things that other feminists would not do. On why she engaged with the media and the inevitable 'cult of personality' that many movement feminists sought to avoid, Greer said 'we have to use whatever weapons we've got'. She saw her role as speaking to the 'unconverted' (Lehrman 1972, 64).

These comments of Greer's could be interpreted as disingenuous, a disguise for her celebrity ambitions. Yet, the topics that Greer chose to discuss in the media – including abortion and rape – suggest greater depth to Greer's feminism than calculated tokenism. Her media engagement throughout 1971 was critical to her taking these discussions to new audiences, and television played an important role in her outreach. Among television audiences, many viewers learned of Greer for the first time after seeing her on late-night television talk shows including those hosted by Johnny Carson, David Frost, David Susskind, and Dick Cavett (Bellamy 1971; F1 1971; F2 1971).

Audience letters responding to Greer's appearance as guest host of *TDCS* reveal the special role that such television talk shows could have in reaching different audiences, humanising feminists, and enabling them to articulate their ideas first hand. As Dow (2014) has argued, although television news helped to broadcast the women's liberation movement to mainstream America, its format did not lend itself to communicating the complexity of radical feminism's big ideas, such as those about patriarchy and social revolution. The television news format of short segments was better suited to communicating liberal feminist campaigns for legislative reform such as equal pay. In contrast, the longer form of the late-night television talk show gave more time for the exploration of ideas. Further, while feminists could be misquoted and otherwise controlled in print, these television talk shows had the potential to give viewers a more complete and direct sense of individual feminists. Although late-night television guests were still framed by the light-hearted tone of the shows, and subject to the presenter's manipulations and network censorship, audiences were nevertheless able to see and hear these guests first hand.

Of all the late-night talk shows, Dick Cavett's show in particular had developed a reputation for featuring topical social and political issues along with the kinds of guests who could talk about them knowledgeably (Timberg 2010, 77). Interestingly though, Cavett had not shown himself to be particularly sympathetic to feminism prior to Greer's turn as guest host of his show. Viewer Mitzi Anderson wrote to Cavett in frustration over his treatment of Germaine Greer and Betty Friedan and said that, as the result, she had stopped watching his show. According to her letter, when Greer first appeared on *TDCS* as a guest, Cavett told her that although he knew of the women's movement he could not 'get interested' in it. When Betty Friedan was his guest, she appeared alongside Victor Borges, a comic pianist who mocked and trivialised all that she said without intervention from Cavett. What hope was there for feminists to be taken seriously when even the most erudite of hosts behaved in this way? (Mitzi Anderson June 11, in F2 1971). The treatment that Anderson's letter describes speaks to the issues feminists generally faced on late-night television: a lack of sympathy from the host coupled with the inability to direct and control the conversation. For *TDCS* and the ABC network, the two episodes with Greer as host were an opportunity to expand content about women and perhaps provide some high-rating entertainment, given Greer's focus on topics related to sex. For Greer, they were a rare chance to run a feminist conversation on her terms, on television.

The guests for Greer's episodes were comprised of political liberals and conservatives, white Americans, and African-Americans. On 14 June, the Monday night that she hosted *TDCS*, Greer discussed birth control. Her diverse panel of guests included Dr David Rorvik, who was in favour of women's right to birth control and abortion; J. Daniel Mahoney, a lawyer and founder of the New York Conservative Party, who argued against abortion for religious reasons and also supported traditional notions of woman-as-mother; Representative Rosetta Ferguson, a Democrat in the Michigan House of Representatives, a Baptist, African-American, and member of the National Association for the Advancement of Colored People, who opposed the legalisation of abortion for religious, moral, and racial reasons (Williams 2016, 192), and Roy Innis, the National Director of the Congress on Racial Equality who, like Ferguson believed that abortion and birth control were tantamount to genocide for black families (Dillard 2001, 9). He also made the critical point that freedom for black women in relation to reproduction was different than freedom for white women. Viewer letters indicate that Greer argued with both Ferguson and Innis over their anti-abortion positions. She appeared unable to see how race figured into considerations of reproductive rights, despite her sympathy for civil rights and people of colour. At the same time, Innis expressed no interest in liberation for white women. He also rejected the need for the liberation of women of colour because, as *Jet* reported of what Innis told Greer, 'Black men and Black women have equal problems' ("New York Beat" 1971). They did not, however, have equal rights as evidenced in Innis' comment that his wife 'belonged to her Daddy and now she belongs to me' (Daly June 14, in F2 1971). It seems that Innis, and perhaps Greer too, failed to recognise that race and gender intersected for women of colour, a failure that feminists of colour sought – and continue to seek – to redress (Springer 2005).

Guests for the next night's episode, in which Greer discussed rape, were Jim Bouton who was a former baseball player for the New York Yankees and had published two books which included discussion of his former teammates' inappropriate sexual behaviour ("Jim Bouton Introduction"); lawyer and prisoner's rights advocate William Hellerstein; writer Sidney Zion; Catholic and Republican William Prendergast, and an unnamed woman who had been raped ("Runsheet for The Dick Cavett Show" 1971).

Greer chose the topics for the two shows she hosted (Daphne Productions 1971). Her choice of topics could be interpreted as being deliberately controversial in order to draw viewers. But restricted access to birth control and the problem of rape were also major feminist issues at a time when abortion was a crime in most US states and rape was shrouded in silence (Echols 1989; Rosen 2001). The way Greer dealt with the topics demonstrated her interest in and feminist commitment to them. During the episode on birth control she argued that every woman should have the right to an abortion because it was a private matter and should not be interfered with by the government, the law, or religious hypocrisy. One viewer of that episode, married 11 years and the mother of two, felt emboldened to write about the abortion she had had earlier that year, and wrote that she was grateful that the option of 'self-determination' was available to her (anon June 15, in F2 1971). Many viewers wrote to thank Greer for the reasonable and open discussion on such a controversial subject (Jenny Chan n.d., in F1 1971). Terry Peters, who wrote from an infantry training unit, disagreed with Greer's position on abortion but still sent a long letter to thank her for airing the conversation (June 15, in F2 1971). Beyond the viewer letters, television reviewer Ben Levine thought that Greer was a model for lifting such 'conversations to a higher level' (Levine 1971).

In the episode about rape, Greer's choice to include a guest who had been the victim of rape reflected the women's liberation movement's argument that the victim's perspective was critical to the definition, understanding, and punishment of rape. But the subject was also personal as Greer herself had been raped (Lehrman 1972; Wallace 1998). It was a subject she discussed in various print interviews, and later wrote about for *Playboy* (Dreifus 1971; Greer 1972). In print, Greer had appeared flippant about being raped, suggesting it had not affected her much. However, the way she handled it on television was entirely different. Viewers commented both that it was an important subject to discuss and that she managed the conversation with great thoughtfulness and sensitivity (Paul R. Sterritt et al., in F1 1971). As the result, one male viewer wrote to say that he had learned a lot about rape (Sam Mandon June 18, in F2 1971). A number of women who had been raped wrote to express their gratitude for the show: one had been raped twice and another had been raped as a child and had helped guide her own daughter through the aftermath of a near rape (anon June 17, in F1 1971). Diane wrote to Greer that 'To be able to discuss rape on television is HEROIC, honest, necessary and an incalculable contribution to a lot of mixed up females'. She was glad, as were others, that Greer had discussed the problems of unsympathetic police and a society that blamed the victims (June 15, in F2 1971).

Jeanne C. Barrett was so affected by the episode that she wrote a letter to Greer and another directly to the ABC network. 'As a persuader', she wrote, '[Greer] is a master engineer. You could see minds and attitudes changing right on stage' (June 16, in F2 1971). Barrett was one of the few writers to note that Greer was an outsider to the United States. Where the mainstream media tended to exoticise Greer as a foreigner – to the extent that Greer was surprised at their 'Anglomania' (Handman, Phillips, and Goldstein 1971) – if the audience acknowledged that she was not American it was in terms of the difference this gave to her analyses. Barrett wrote that

> By presenting rape as the manifestation of our attitudes toward sex, men, and women, she did this society a service. It leaves no doubt as to how we see ourselves. We are a brutalised people, and a Germaine Greer is not only necessary to point this out, but to supply us with a model to follow as well.

A self-identified feminist also wrote to express the United States' need for Greer:

> Since the attitude of society toward rape is indicative of its attitude toward women, it is a subject of more than casual interest to all feminists, as I am sure you know. The fact that this is the only major country where women can move around freely only in the daytime for fear of being attacked is disgraceful. WE need you here much more than England does! Last night at a local meeting of the National Organization for Women, there was much praise for your programs [on *TDCS*] and the ones who missed them were so unhappy that I wondered if it might be possible to get tapes of these programs (Martha E. Gresham June 17, in F2 1971).

Such enthusiastic responses were typical. Across approximately 400 letters, about 80% of viewer letters concerning Greer's *TDCS* episodes were overwhelmingly positive. A dominant theme of the letters was about the depth of the conversation and coverage of the issues, something that many viewers commented was rare on television generally and that positively differentiated *TDCS* from its late-night competitors. Mrs Sue Penunuri wrote that there was a need for more such 'honest and realistic programs', a sentiment shared by many viewers (June 19, in F2 1971). Although many of the letters linked this achievement to Greer, many of them were addressed to *TDCS* and to the ABC, and congratulated them for the 'genius' idea of getting Greer to host the show and for allowing her to discuss such issues (Ruth Friedlander June 14, in F2 1971). Lynn Owens (n.d., in F2 1971) wrote that it was 'refreshing to hear the opinions and views from the "other side" after too many superficial (and many times chauvinistic) talk show hosts have passed by on the 'ole TV set'. To Jim Klaslerboe, Greer was leading important conversations 'that will save this country from itself' (June 16, in F2 1971). Greer's appearance thus gave cachet to the show and the television network.

The depth of discussion reflected well on Greer, too. A few of the viewers were surprised to learn that Greer had 'depth' after the superficial portrayals of her in articles such as the *Life* cover story that portrayed her as the 'saucy feminist that even men like' (Bonfante 1971). Jeanne C. Barrett wrote to Greer: 'Life magazine claims your appeal is that you "like men." I claim that your appeal is that your intellect is welded to a very handsome ability to communicate' (June 16, in F2 1971). This transformed perception of Greer was in fact shared by some feminists who, on meeting Greer, were surprised to find that she 'was superb – her wit and articulation impressed the hell out of us and it was clear that she is a "sister"' (Sheila 1971). In comparing these television viewer responses to Greer with the experience some feminists had of meeting Greer in person, it is possible to get the sense that television conveyed Greer's ideas and personality more fully than the print media had done.

Still, a number of the letters noted the way in which television appeared to mediate and censor Greer. Some viewers commented that, unlike her guests, Greer was not introduced by name and they either still did not know who she was or they had to call the network to find out. More worrying to some though, Greer's two episodes on the Monday and Tuesday nights were followed on the Wednesday night with a re-run of a *TDCS* episode from earlier in the year. Many viewers expressed concern that Greer had been cut from the show after the episode on rape for being too controversial. There is no evidence that Greer had been scheduled for more than two episodes, but viewers received the impression that she had been cut because the network had censored the guest William Hellerstein's discussion of sexual perversion. Viewers were concerned too that a guest's comments had damned Greer's future on the show. At the end of the episode about rape, Jim Bouton criticised Greer on air for what he thought was her poor job of hosting the show. Bouton said he believed that television hosts should be 'superficial' and that Greer was not what a female host should be: 'light, witty and cute' (Janie Damminger n.d., in F2 1971).

Some agreed with Jim Bouton's assessment of Greer as inappropriate for television hosting and went further, criticising everything from her 'gaudy' attire, unkempt hair, and failure to wear a bra, to her 'obnoxious' demeanour and rude treatment of her guests (Phyllis A. Polley June 15, in F2 1971; Mr and Mrs Jesse Clifford June 16, in F1 1971). Some viewers thought that Greer had gone far beyond her role as moderator and had stifled and dominated opinions that differed from her own (Mrs Henry Cosevya June 14, in F1 1971; Willie Mae Etheridge n.d., in F2 1971). Mrs Wardell N. Weeden called her a 'pompous ass who has no business sitting in the interviewer's seat' (June 14, in F2 1971). Others found Greer overly analytical to the degree that 'she analyses sex until there is nothing left of it, certainly no fun – or even pleasure' (Anne Duncan June 19, in F2 1971). These criticisms reveal much about the expectations of female propriety, including a neat and attractive appearance, deference to the opinions of others, and an emotional rather than logical bearing.

Interestingly, the clear majority of negative letters about Germaine Greer were from women. This speaks to the role that women played as gatekeepers of traditional womanhood and associated morality (Ehrenreich, Hess, and Jacobs 1986; McGirr 2001). That some viewers perceived Greer as an affront to these traditions was evident in a letter from Bea

Richards who wrote angrily to Dick Cavett: 'The only good thing I can say about [her] is that [she] probably set the Women's Lib movement back'. Her postscript noted: 'I am not for Women's Lib! I'm a successful wife (32 years) and mother of 3 and grandmother of 3 – and proud of it!' (June 21, in F1 1971). Bea Richards' comments are telling in their suggestion that marriage and motherhood were incompatible with women's liberation, as feminists such as Germaine Greer were indeed arguing. By implication, Greer represented a threat to traditional womanhood, the containment of female sexuality, and the traditional family. This threat was at the heart of viewer criticisms directed at her. Indeed, a number of the negative viewer responses connected Greer's position on liberated female sexuality with a 'cheap' lack of morality (Meg L. June 16, in F2 1971). Others described Greer as 'disgusting' (Helen Francis June 17, in F2 1971; Marian Murphy June 16, in F2 1971), and as looking like 'a worn-out whore' (Rod Martin June 18, in F2 1971). One wished a 'social disease' on Greer (Al Rose n.d., in F2 1971) and another went so far as to say that Greer was so revolting that, barring 'immaculate conception' she would never have to face abortion (Mrs Norman Dillon June 14, in F2 1971).

Still, a far greater volume of the letters refuted Jim Bouton's analysis of Greer and supported Greer's ideas and the kind of femininity she embodied. Indeed, the majority of letter writers saw Greer as a positive model of non-traditional womanhood. In their comments on Greer's qualities, the letters indicate the types of women that viewers were used to seeing on television – 'dumb blondes' as one viewer described them. In contrast, Greer challenged female stereotypes. Many viewers commented on Greer's rare candour, intelligence, and wit, even when they did not entirely agree with her (Joan Neff June 14, in F2 1971). These were atypical characteristics for most television hosts, they noted, and were all the more striking because Greer was a woman. As Margaret and Steven Karis wrote, Greer 'demonstrated the fact that women can be articulate and intelligent; and brought an unsurpassed degree of honesty to television' (June 15, in F2 1971). Jackie Daly – who identified herself as sympathetic to the women's movement and its goals, although she was not a member of a liberation group – thought Greer was 'an outstanding refutation to the myth that women are not logical and cannot go through a discussion of an emotion-charged issue, such as abortion reform, without sticking to calm, reasonable debate' (June 14, in F2 1971).

Greer inspired male and female viewers because of these qualities. Mark Warner, who described himself as 'a 17 year-old white male of middle class parents, living in a small rural town …' wrote to Greer that her 'tact and depth' had given him much to think about. 'As an aspiring intellect,' he wrote, 'I can't say enough about how much I respect you' (June 16, in F2 1971). 80-Year-old Emily Dumont wrote to Greer to say 'I think you are tops' (June 6, in F2 1971). Agnes Carlin admired Greer's ability to stay calm during heated debate and expressed her desire for Greer to continue to be such a positive role model for women (June 15, in F2 1971). A number of the letter writers shared Lisa Lowe's sentiment to Greer: 'You made me feel proud to be female' (16 June, in F2 1971).

Many viewers were pleased that Greer had the forum to positively communicate about women's issues and thought that she was a great spokesperson for women. One of the women who wrote to comment on the abortion discussion also wrote that: 'It is a fresh breeze to hear the taboo words of menstruation, ovulation etc. discussed in open conversation. The import to individual women of now being included in polite conversation that goes somewhere is immense' (anon June 15, in F2 1971). Josephine Cuerpo wrote that

Greer was 'one of the few brilliant women getting the spotlight in this country' (June 14, in F2 1971). Goldie Beer wrote to Greer that she 'must be the most articulate, charming and literate exponent for change ... helping to enlighten the public today' (June 18, in F2 1971). A 21-year-old male viewer wrote that if more women like Greer were given such a platform, then there would be more chance of women's issues being taken seriously (Harris Snoparsky, in F1 1971). Similarly, Sandra Rosenbergh believed that if there were more women like Greer, presenting with a 'non-coy straightforward manner', 'we would no longer be the unheard majority' (June 21, in F1 1971). Indeed, Jeanette Thompson wrote: 'It is so far past time for someone to speak up for women and out against all the indignities our sex is expected to "suffer in silence" ... And speak well she does' (June 14, in F2 1971). Betty Powell described Greer as 'a magnificent human being' who was a boon for 'the struggle to help women realize their full potential' (June 15, in F2 1971).

Some viewers strongly identified with Greer. Jamie Damminger wrote to her:

> I feel you're a beautiful sister! [emphasis in original] Just after having watched you both nights I feel very close to you. I feel very strongly your concern about me as a woman as I too have this desire of freedom for all my sisters. (n.d., in F2 1971)

In a tenderly expressed identification that spoke to the hope and liberating possibilities Greer signified, Eugenia Plunkett wrote: 'I hold my breath watching the fledgling of me and all women in you' (n.d., in F2 1971).

A number of viewers gained new understanding of women's liberation and were won over to the cause by Greer. Ann Meyer learned from Greer that women's liberation was much deeper than what she had gleaned from the media (June 17, in F2 1971). Another wrote, 'thank you for opening up my mind to the real crux of women's lib' (Carolyn Laine June 16, in F2 1971). A man named Walter wrote with gratitude that Greer had 'greatly affected my views on the subject of female liberation' and that Greer had 'greatly increased my own understanding of myself and my relationship to the opposite sex' (June 16, in F2 1971). Other viewers thought that Greer was an ideal exponent of feminism. One wrote: 'Women's Lib. spokesmen [sic] usually have me writhing in embarrassment whereas Miss Greer is an example for us all to emulate' (Mrs Juliet Fowler June 15, in F2 1971). Another wrote that Greer's 'points and ideas are the ones that many females of my generation (21 yr old) are in agreement with, rather than those of the gung-ho women's liberation activists ... .' (Bonnie J. Thompson June 15, in F2 1971).

It is interesting to consider which of Greer's qualities appealed more than those of other feminists to these viewers. Perhaps they were similar to those identified by the mainstream media: her charisma, beauty, and heterosexuality. These qualities may have made Greer more acceptable than feminists who challenged all aspects of mainstream femininity, along the lines of Susan Douglas's reflection that Greer, and Gloria Steinem, 'made [her] feel that women could cobble together elements of the codes of femininity they were unable to expunge with a feminism they were eager to adopt' (Douglas 1995, 232). Viewers were also comparing, perhaps unfairly and unevenly, Greer's version of feminism as presented on a late-night television talk show, when she was in charge of the conversation, with the mediated and more two-dimensional ideas of feminists they got from the print media and television news.

Most of the letters do not comment explicitly on why Greer seemed more appealing than other feminists. A few viewers, mostly male, commented on Greer's attractiveness, while others, even those who were won over by her, commented that the appeal of her intelligence and ideas was undermined by her unkempt appearance. The majority of positive commentary said nothing about Greer's appearance or sexuality. That does not mean that these qualities were not factors in her appeal, whether conscious or unconscious. Greer represented key features of dominant womanhood: she was white, heterosexual, and cis-gendered. So perhaps she veered far enough from the established script of traditional womanhood to inspire, but not far enough to alienate the majority of the viewing audience.

For minority viewers, Greer appeared differently. As one wrote, she did not dislike Greer on *TDCS* but wished that a 'young black woman' like herself, would be invited onto the show to express her views on the black woman's role and standpoint in the women's liberation movement 'or even better to engage in a debate with' Greer (Carolyn Tyler June 21, in F2 1971). This woman's letter points beyond Greer to the whiteness of second-wave feminism as broadcast and produced by the media and by some white feminists (Hesford 2013). The singularity of her letter speaks also to what may have been a predominantly white viewing audience for *TDCS*.[2] It is important to bear this in mind when considering the extent to which this audience might be representative of the American public more broadly.

In response to the many letters that called for Greer's return to the show, Cavett's company, Daphne Productions, proposed to create for Greer a show of her own. A draft proposal for it summarised many of the letters in commenting that Greer 'brought a new excitement to the role of the female as host of a television program [which] proved that the "coffee-klatch" [sic] kind of conversation that the medium has imposed upon its women hosts is ... out of date ... .' (Daphne Productions 1971). The show did not eventuate, and it is unclear from the available sources whether that decision was made by Greer or by the predominantly male network executives at ABC.[3] It is interesting to consider what the past and present of feminism might have looked like if Greer had appeared on her own television talk show in the 1970s. Would her show have become a focal and rallying point for the 'unheard majority' who identified themselves in the audience letters? Could it have helped to build a powerful pro-feminist community of ordinary Americans?

The fact that Greer was so well-received by a mainstream audience is at odds with the image of her that we get from published print sources written by feminists and the mainstream media. These print sources portray Greer as a woman who fit traditional notions of feminine beauty and heterosexual availability even as she transgressed expected passivity, and who betrayed what some of her feminist sisters thought was the best way to achieve their goals. In feminist critiques of Greer, her willingness to work with the media helped to establish negative images of feminists, and thus compromised the understanding and uptake of feminism.

The implied audience in histories drawn from these published sources is a passive one whose opinion of second-wave feminism was of one mind with, or uncritically shaped by, the media and other reactionary forces. In turn, the media sought to maintain traditional womanhood and patriarchal power by promoting their 'chosen' feminist. Certainly, Greer's charisma, heterosexuality, and whiteness played a role in her appeal to the media and to members of the public. She did not stray from the race, sexuality or gender identity of the dominant image of womanhood. Nor, in wearing make-up and fashionable clothing, did she reject all the trappings of traditional femininity.

Still, Greer did not represent the traditional or typical woman, and the actual viewing audience appreciated that. Their letters tell us that it was Greer's intelligence, rationality, wit and strength of character that made her so appealing and such an effective communicator. The majority of her audience perceived her as giving a face to these long-ignored and denied female qualities, and they embraced the expanded possibilities for womanhood that she embodied. The letters provide evidence that Greer's media engagement was critical to the mainstream dissemination of her ideas about feminism and feminist consciousness-raising. Through Greer, feminism moved from the theoretical realm to the worlds of everyday people, where it had the potential to make a real difference. In addition to the organised feminists who led the changes, these people helped to support positive change in the lives of American women, including on the issues of abortion and rape.

The evidence that Greer was so well-received by a mainstream audience creates a productive tension with the feminists who discounted her efficacy. The tension invites us to dig into the archives, to write expanded and more nuanced histories of second-wave feminism and its reception, and to remember that movements do not operate in a vacuum. It also raises questions. If the public were more receptive to feminism than has been commonly believed, how can we better understand resistance to feminism, and, trace throughlines for its support? In the absence of archival sources, how might we recognise and identify the gaps in recorded history? In considering contemporary feminist activism, Greer's importance as a spokesperson for feminism points to the need for different feminists to fulfil different roles in a movement – and the need to find a way to recognise and accommodate these differences rather than be fractured by them.

The letters that Germaine Greer carefully collected and preserved are witness to her impact in the United States. In the force of their comments and the very fact that the letters were written – many explained that this was the first time they had been inspired to write a letter – these viewers tell us how extraordinary it was to see a woman such as Germaine Greer on American television in 1971, and how much seeing her meant to them. Greer has commented that she is 'probably the least interesting part of my archive' ("Germaine speaks" 2013) and it is true that these letters tell us about more than Greer. These letters give us insight into the everyday lives of the audience members who wrote them, lives where they tuned in to television programs – and other broadcast media – that were limited and limiting in their depictions of womanhood, programs that typically gave no space to discussion of the serious issues women grappled with daily. In the letters, we hear the voices of ordinary people usually silenced by the production of history, voices that tell of how they, along with feminists and the mainstream media, understood the meanings of feminism and shaped its past and its future.

Notes

1. I note that while some footage of other *TDCS* guests is available online, there appears to be no readily available footage of Greer's appearances on *TDCS* and I have been unable to watch the episodes. This absence speaks to the importance of Greer's archive for feminist history.
2. One other letter expressed interest in the black standpoint. Pam Brick wrote to say that she had enjoyed Greer, as much for the important subjects she discussed as for her intelligence

and competence. She suggested that at some stage 'a sincere member of the black community' be asked to guest host for *TDCS* (June 14, in F2 1971).
3. Julie D'Acci (1994) has written about the struggles that the television show *Cagney & Lacey* had with its network due to its two female leads and feminist content despite its high ratings.

Acknowledgements

I am grateful to the special editors of this issue, particularly Maryanne Dever, the anonymous reviewers, Rachel Buchanan, Zora Simic, Anthony Sheehan, and Anwen Crawford for their encouragement, comments, suggestions, and help. Thanks to Sophie Langley and Emmet Gillespie for their research assistance. This article is dedicated to Joy with the green eyes and the brilliant mind, who has lived her feminist life with remarkable dignity and grace, who has shown me all the love of a fairy godmother, and who brings all these qualities, and more, to helping raise Reyna Joy, the next generation.

Disclosure statement

No potential conflict of interest was reported by the author.

References

Armstrong, John. 2006. "Applying Critical Theory to Electronic Media History." In *Methods of Historical Analysis in Electronic Media*, edited by Donald G. Godfrey, 145–166. Mahwah, NJ: Lawrence Erlbaum Associates.
Bellamy, Harmon. 1971. "The Book Nook," *Jewish Weekly News*, December 16. University of Melbourne Archives, Germaine Greer Archive, 2014.0038, Box 217, "Press, USA, 1971".
Bonfante, Jordan. 1971. "Germaine Greer." *Life*, May 7, 30–33.
Cadden, Vivian. 1972. "Women's Lib? I've Seen It on TV." *Redbook*, February, 89–96.
Cantwell, Mary. 1971. "An Opinion: Thoughts After an Evening with Norman Mailer, Germaine Greer, Diana Trilling, Jill Johnston, Jacqueline Ceballos and a Cast of Thousands." *Mademoiselle*, July, 36, 38, 40.
Cohen, Marcia. 1988. *The Sisterhood: The True Story of the Women Who Changed the World*. New York: Simon and Schuster.
D'Acci, Julie. 1994. *Defining Women: Television and the Case of Cagney & Lacey*. Chapel Hill: University of North Carolina Press.
Daphne Productions. 1971. "The Germaine Greer Show: A Presentation." University of Melbourne Archives, Germaine Greer Archive, 2014.0038, Box 218, "Germaine Greer Show 'pitch' NY 1971."
Dillard, Angela D. 2001. *Guess Who's Coming to Dinner Now? Multicultural Conservatism in America*. New York: New York University Press.
Douglas, Susan J. 1995. *Where the Girls Are: Growing Up Female with the Mass Media*. New York: Time Books.

Dow, Bonnie J. 2014. *Watching Women's Liberation, 1970: Feminism's Pivotal Year on the Network News*. Urbana: University of Illinois Press.

Dreifus, Claudia. 1971. "Freeing Women's Sexuality: An Interview with Germaine Greer." *Evergreen Review* 25–27: 50–54.

Dreifus, Claudia. [1971] 1973. "The Selling of Feminism." Reprinted In *Radical Feminism*, edited by Anne Koedt, Ellen Levine, & Anita Rapone, 358–361. New York: Quadrangle Books.

Echols, Alice. 1989. *Daring to Be Bad: Radical Feminism in America 1967–1975*. Minneapolis: University of Minnesota Press.

Ehrenreich, Barbara, Elizabeth Hess, and Gloria Jacobs. 1986. *Re-Making Love: The Feminization of Sex*. New York: Anchor Books.

Eichhorn, Kate. 2013. *The Archival Turn in Feminism: Outrage in Order*. Philadelphia, PA: Temple University Press.

Engelhardt, Molly. 2003. "'Airheads, Amazons, and Bitches' Cheerleaders and Second-Wave Feminists in the Popular Press." In *Disco Divas*, edited by Sherrie A. Inness, 54–68. Philadelphia: University of Pennsylvania Press.

F1. 1971. University of Melbourne Archives, Germaine Greer Archive, 2014.0038, Box 218, "Audience Response to GG."

F2. 1971. University of Melbourne Archives, Germaine Greer Archive, 2014.0038, Box 218, "Audience Response to GG (2)."

"The Female Eunuch." *Newsweek*, March 22, 1971, 48.

"The Female Eunuch." *Seattle Post-Intelligencer*. University of Melbourne Archives, Germaine Greer Archive, 2014.0038, Box 217, "Press, USA, 1971."

Foote, Timothy. 1972. "Lib and Let Lib." *Time*, March 20, 100.

"Germaine Greer Speaks at the Opening of the 'Protest! Archives from the University of Melbourne' Exhibition at The University of Melbourne Library." 2013. Accessed February 15, 2016. https://www.youtube.com/watch?v=ppRX1XuCO8w.

"Germaine Greer Tells of Media Bias." *Daily World*, May 28, 1971. "Germaine Greer articles and clippings." Women's Liberation Collection, Sophia Smith Collection, Smith College, Northampton, MA.

Greenfield, Robert. 1971. "A Groupie in Women's Lib." *Rolling Stone*, January 7, 17.

Greer, Germaine. 1972. "Seduction is a Four-Letter Word." *Playboy*, January, 80–82, 164, 178, 224, 226–228.

Handman, Heidi, Mary Phillips, and Al Goldstein. 1971. "Part Two: The Greering of America: Feminism for Fun and Profit." *Screw Magazine*, May 31, 8–12.

Hesford, Victoria. 2013. *Feeling Women's Liberation*. Durham: Duke University Press.

Izzo, Amanda. 2002. "Outrageous and Everyday: The Papers of Gloria Steinem." *Journal of Women's History* 14 (2): 151–153.

"Jim Bouton Introduction Card." n.d. University of Melbourne Archives, Germaine Greer Archive, 2014.0038, Box 218, "Germaine Greer Show 'pitch' NY 1971."

Johnston, Jill. 1971. "Germaine & Guillaume in Baltimore." *Village Voice*, April 22, 31–32.

Johnston, Jill. 1998. *Admission Accomplished: The Lesbian Nation Years (1970–75)*. London: Serpent's Tail.

Kempton, Sally. 1971. "The Female Eunuch." *New York Times*, April 15. https://www.nytimes.com/books/99/05/09/specials/greer-eunuch.html.

Koedt, Anne, and Shulamith Firestone. 1971. *Notes from the Third Year: Women's Liberation*. New York. http://library.duke.edu/digitalcollections/wlmpc_wlmms01038_wlmms010380020/.

Koedt, Anne, Ellen Levine, and Anita Rapone, eds. 1973. *Radical Feminism*. New York: Quadrangle Books.

Lehmann-Haupt, Christopher. 1970. "He and She II." *New York Times*, August 6, 31.

Lehmann-Haupt, Christopher. 1971. "The Best Feminist Book So Far." *New York Times*, April 20, 41.

Lehrman, Nat. 1972. "Playboy Interview: Germaine Greer." *Playboy*, January, 61–64, 66, 68, 70, 72, 74, 76, 78, 80, 82.

Levine, Ben. 1971. "TV: Germaine Greer." *Individual Woman*, June 17, 8. "Germaine Greer Articles and Clippings." Women's Liberation Collection, Sophia Smith Collection, Smith College, Northampton, MA.

Levine, Elana. 2007. "Sex as a Weapon: Programming Sexuality in the 1970s." In *NBC: America's Network*, edited by Michele Hilmes and Michael Henry, 224–239. Berkeley: University of California Press.

McGirr, Lisa. 2001. *Suburban Warriors: The Origins of the New American Right*. Princeton, NJ: Princeton University Press.

"New York Beat." 1971. *Jet*, July 8, 61.

Reed, Evelyn. 1971. "Feminism and 'The Female Eunuch.'" *International Socialist Review*, July–August, 10, 12–13, 31–36.

Rosen, Ruth. 2001. *The World Split Open: How the Modern Women's Movement Changed America*. New York: Penguin Books.

"Runsheet for The Dick Cavett Show for June 15, 1971," n.d. University of Melbourne Archives, Germaine Greer Archive, 2014.0038, Box 218, "Germaine Greer Show 'pitch' NY 1971."

Sheila (Editorial Rooms *Rampart* magazine). 1971. "Letter to Susan (at Suck magazine)." University of Melbourne Archives, Germaine Greer Archive, 2014.0038, Box 219, "Suck correspondence 1971," June 28, 1971.

Smith, Nathan. 2015. "Feminist Artifacts: The Archive of Germaine Greer." *Los Angeles Review of Books*, March 21. Accessed February 15, 2016. https://lareviewofbooks.org/essay/feminist-artifacts-archive-germaine-greer/.

Spongberg, Mary. 1993. "If She's So Great, How Come So Many Pigs Dig Her? Germaine Greer and the Malestream Press." *Women's History Review* 2 (3): 407–418.

Springer, Kimberly. 2005. *Living for the Revolution: Black Feminist Organizations, 1968–1980*. Durham: Duke University Press.

Taylor, Anthea. 2014. "Germaine Greer's Adaptable Celebrity." *Feminist Media Studies* 14 (5): 759–774. doi:10.1080/14680777.2013.810165.

Timberg, Bernard M. 2010. *Television Talk: A History of the TV Talk Show*. Austin: University of Texas Press.

Wallace, Christine. 1998. *Germaine Greer: Untamed Shrew*. New York: Faber and Faber.

Weinraub, Judith. 1971. "Opinions That May Shock the Faithful." *New York Times*, March 22, 28.

Williams, Daniel K. 2016. *Defenders of the Unborn: The Pro-Life Movement Before Roe v. Wade*. New York: Oxford University Press.

Withorn, Ann. 1971. "Book Reviews." *Harvard Educational Review*. University of Melbourne Archives, Germaine Greer Archive, 2014.0038, Box 217, "Press, USA, 1971."

"Women's Liberation." 1971. *Pioneer Woman*, December. University of Melbourne Archives, Germaine Greer Archive, 2014.0038, Box 217, "Press, USA, 1971."

A feminist fashion icon: Germaine Greer's paisley coat

Petra Mosmann

ABSTRACT
This article concerns Germaine Greer's paisley coat, featured in *Vogue* and *Life* magazines in May 1971. Focusing on the coat disrupts how we locate Greer as a subject and women's liberation as an event. The article explores the intersection of fashion and feminist movements by analysing Greer's coat, its archive and by placing the coat in a conversation with Greer's thoughts on fashion. Women's liberation's relationship with fashion has primarily been remembered through anti-fashion and anti- beauty protests. The making, wearing and display of Greer's coat challenges simple categorisations of both Greer and feminism's history.

In 2010, Germaine Greer presented her paisley coat and a shawl fragment to the National Museum of Australia (NMA) in Canberra. Greer sewed the coat herself in 1969, using fabric cut from the shawl. She wore it for several years, notably for photographs published in *Life* and *Vogue* magazine in 1971, and during her American book tour promoting *The Female Eunuch*. Greer's coat is an example of late 1960s and early 1970s counter-culture fashion. Since December 2013, the coat and shawl fragment have been on display at the NMA (Figures 1 and 2). The same cabinet exhibiting Greer's coat also features dresses worn by Miss Australia contestant winners from 1961 and 1962 (Figures 3–5). For me, viewing Greer's coat alongside a display about the Miss Australia competition prompted questions about the place of fashion in transnational memories of women's liberation. This article explores the intersection of fashion and feminist movements by analysing Greer's coat, assembling her coat's 'archive',[1] and exploring how Greer approaches fashion. Whether Greer is understood as an anti-fashion feminist or presented as a feminist fashion icon matters, as what is at stake here is how we remember and narrate feminism's history.

When feminists write about the relationship between fashion and feminism, and cite Greer in particular, they tend to do so in order to make a specific point. Feminists often cite Greer's thoughts on fashion in order to imply that 1970s feminists had (and still have) a troubling approach to fashion that must be overcome or remedied in someway (Church-Gibson 2000, 349–353; Edwards 2011, 67–85; Scott 2005, 301; Beckingham 2005, 14; 229). Greer has a complex and evolving relationship with fashion, but this is never explored or contextualised. Feminist fashion scholar Pamela Church-Gibson has the most sustained and wide ranging engagement with Greer's thoughts on fashion. I

Figure 1. Germaine Greer exhibition at the National Museum of Australia (Photograph by Petra Mosmann).

therefore turn to her specific narration of Greer, as it demonstrates the importance of paying attention to the way particular narratives locate feminist subjects, events and schools of thought (Hemmings 2011, 5).

In 2000, Church-Gibson reflected on the past, present and future intersections of fashion and the feminist movement. At the time, she was troubled by contemporary feminist hostility towards fashion, but also wary of feminist approaches that uncritically celebrate fashion (349–350). She cites Greer as representative of contemporary feminist hostility, stating that 'Greer has been the dominant figure in defining feminist anti fashion rhetoric' since the publication of *The Female Eunuch* (350). At the time, Greer

Figure 2. Germaine Greer exhibition at the National Museum of Australia (Photograph by Petra Mosmann).

had just published *The Whole Woman* (1999), which includes a sustained critique of contemporary fashion and beauty practices. Greer had also relatively recently made negative, well publicised comments about Suzanne Moore's shoes, dress and lipstick choices (Church-Gibson 2000, 351; Edwards 2011, 82). Church-Gibson (2000, 351) reflects:

> This attack [on Suzanne Moore] is—paradoxically—misogynist in its tone and reminiscent of the strident puritanism around dress that characterised Anglo-American feminism in the late 1960s and early 1970s. Indeed it has never really gone away … Obviously, every emergent political force is likely to be purist … the new, diverse feminisms in the West have no need to proclaim their identity by the imposition of uniforms.

Figure 3. Germaine Greer exhibition at the National Museum of Australia (Photograph by Petra Mosmann).

Although Greer's commentary on high profile women's dress practices is sometimes troubling,[2] this response from Church-Gibson is problematic in several respects.[3] It positions Greer and Greer's critique of fashion as unchanging and representative of late 1960s and early 1970s feminist approaches.[4] It implies that in the late 1960s and early 1970s feminists did not engage with or debate approaches to fashion. But what I am most interested in here is the way Church-Gibson's citation of Greer locates women's liberation as a naive but necessary stage in feminism's development. It locates Greer and Greer's contemporary criticisms of fashion as an anachronism. The statement demonstrates how affective narratives mobilise discussions about fashion and feminism. In her chapter, Church-Gibson

Figure 4. Germaine Greer exhibition at the National Museum of Australia (Photograph by Petra Mosmann).

Figure 5. Germaine Greer exhibition at the National Museum of Australia (Photograph by Petra Mosmann).

(2000) specifically presents what Hemmings (2011, 4–5) calls the 'return' narrative, as she narrates 1970s feminists as naively unified, and implies that poststructuralist approaches have diversified feminist approaches to fashion; however, she ultimately argues that a feminist materialist approach is necessary to make it possible for feminist fashion theory to examine fashion critically. She suggests that we oscillate between the 'celebration and repudiation' of fashion (Church-Gibson, 361).

Rather than being specific to Church-Gibson or fashion studies, this is illustrative of an ongoing issue Western feminist theory generally has with the narration of feminist movements. Hemmings (2011, 3) asserts that despite 'the complexity of the last few decades of feminist theory ... the story of its past is consistently told as a series of interlocking narratives of progress, loss and return'. These narratives oversimplify feminism's history and 'position feminist subjects as needing to inhabit a theoretical and cutting edge in the present' (Hemmings 2011, 3). Feminist writing on fashion produces specific versions of these interlocking narratives identified by Hemmings; in each version, women's liberationists must be positioned as united in their critique of the fashion system. Focusing on Greer's paisley coat disrupts how we tend to locate Greer as a subject and women's liberation as an event.

To clarify, in this article I want to avoid assessing the viability of Greer's approach to fashion. Rather, I consider how narrations of women's liberation are animated by the relationship between fashion and feminist movements. In this article, I make three specific interventions around Greer's coat and her engagement with fashion. First, I analyse the presentation of Greer's coat in *Vogue* and *Life* magazines, as it was the coat's inclusion in these publications that make it a particularly collectable and significant object. Both *Vogue* and *Life* present Greer as a fashionable feminist; however, framing Greer in this way relies on the presentation of her heterosexuality. Second, I outline how Greer's coat demonstrates that her critique of fashion in the 1970s was embodied, creative and often employed parody. Women's liberation's relationship with fashion has primarily been remembered through anti-fashion and anti-beauty protests. The coat embodies 1970s counter cultural protest, rather than being 'outside' the fashion system or subservient to it, the coat was part of creating a fashion trend. Finally, I return to Greer's coat at the NMA, which is placed alongside a display about Miss Australia and Miss International contestants. Rather than narrating the Australian women's liberation movement, this placement evokes Greer as an international feminist celebrity, and challenges how we remember feminist movements and beauty competitions. It also implicitly evokes the nexus established in *Life* and *Vogue* magazines, between heterosexuality, the fashionable and humour.

The making of a fashion icon: *Vogue* and *Life*, May 1971

In May 1971, both *Vogue* (UK) and *Life* magazines featured images of Greer wearing her homemade paisley coat and presented her as a fashionable feminist. *Vogue* (May 1971, 125) included a smouldering black and white photo portrait of Greer, taken by Lord Snowdon, which is now held by the National Portrait Gallery in the UK.[5] The principal photograph depicts Greer sitting on a beanbag in a pair of low-heeled knee-high boots, wearing a skirt, scarf and the paisley patterned coat. She wears make up and her eyebrows form two perfect slightly arched lines. The walls around her are covered in accessories, necklaces, bags and scarves. She maintains a neutral expression. The second photograph featured by *Vogue* (May 1971, 126–127) is more playful than the first. Greer wears the same clothes, but rather than presenting a deadpan expression, she is shown laughing. These photographs are not out of place in *Vogue* magazine's high fashion pages.

In the same month, Greer appeared on the cover of *Life* Magazine and was presented as 'the saucy feminist that even men like' (May 7, 1971). Bonfante (1971, 30) describes Greer as looking 'like a singer of country rock. Imposing, tall and attractive she wears a long buckskin shirt, clogs on her feet, bangles and beads and other hippie accoutrements'. For the cover of *Life* Greer dressed in contrasting colours, in bright red shoes, a blue dress, blue stockings and the same paisley patterned coat worn in *Vogue*. In the colour image the coat glows red and orange in the sunlight. The *Life* article also features four black and white photographs of Greer. One photograph shows her joining a peace march in Washington; a women's liberation badge is prominently pinned to the paisley coat. Another photo playfully presents her alone in the countryside, collecting firewood, wearing a tight leather jacket and knee length skirt. A smaller image shows her teaching a class at Warwick University. The final full page image in the article is explicitly heterosexual, as Greer is photographed cradling Dick Fontaine, an English friend and filmmaker who visited her in New York. Given that Greer often parodied fashion in her writing practices, it seems possible that this was her intention when posing for *Vogue* and *Life*.[6] The images of Greer emphasise that feminism is pleasurable, sexually liberating, stylish and has a sense of humour. However, this nexus is produced in a specific historical context, as *Vogue* and *Life's* presentation of Greer as a fashionable, attractive and funny feminist celebrity is tied to American feminist Kate Millett's public statement about her bisexuality, and the emergence of the 'feminist-as-lesbian figure' in public cultures.[7]

In August 1970, *Time* magazine celebrated Millett's *Sexual Politics* and named her the 'high priestess' of feminism. However, as Hesford's (2013, 62–63) research on the American women's liberation movement demonstrates, by December 1970 the press had already turned on Millett.[8] An article titled 'Women's Lib: A Second Look', published in *Time* magazine on the 14 December 1970 attacks Millett in particular and women's liberationists generally. The article uses Millett's 'confession' of bisexuality to caricature women's liberationists as a group of man-hating, psychologically damaged, bra burning, unattractive lesbians (Hesford 2013, 25–77). She uses this article in *Time* to argue that it was this particular moment in 1970 that the 'feminist-as-lesbian figure' fully emerged in the press and popular culture. This occurred only a few months before Greer was featured by *Vogue* and *Life*. In her study, Hesford implies but does not draw attention to the way 1970s feminist relationships with fashion were shaped by the emergence of the feminist-as-lesbian figure. By praising Greer's publication and presenting her as a funny, fashionable feminist, *Vogue* and *Life* are able to celebrate women's liberation while simultaneously vilifying emerging lesbian feminisms and feminist criticisms of fashion. Presenting Greer as fashionable is central, rather than peripheral to this process, as is demonstrated by the following close analysis of the features included in *Vogue* and *Life*.

When *Vogue* (UK) invited Greer to be photographed in 1971, they also invited Millett, but she declined the invitation. Despite this, a small smiley photograph of Millett is still included in the issue's pages. This inclusion is crucial to the way Greer is positioned in Vogue. *Vogue* highlights that: 'She [Millett] refused to see *Vogue* because: "such magazines perpetuate an oppressive even rather dehumanising image of women as objects of ornament rather than as persons'" (Tynan 1971, 127). The article, written by Tynan (1971, 124–127), was titled 'Germaine Greer ... and Kate Millett'. The article is structured on the page to emphasise the ellipses. Comparisons of Millett and Greer were not uncommon following the publication of *The Female Eunuch* (Spongberg 1993, 409). In Tynan's article, an explicit comparison of Greer and Millett's bodies, sexuality, voice and dress is intertwined with Tynan's assessment of their respective publications. Tynan (1971, 124) opens by flatteringly describing Greer's appearance: '32, just under 6 ft tall, boldly dressed and bra-less, with a long Pre-Raphaelite face, and a voice that can be coaxingly soft or stridently vulgar ... ' Tynan then positively reviews *The Female Eunuch,* calling it 'intelligent', 'beautifully written' and 'deeply subversive' (124). Tynan describes Millett quite differently, as 'reserved', 'sharp-witted' and describes *Sexual Politics* as 'erudite', but then goes on to critique Millett's writing style and calls her a 'hard liner', comparing her with Greer who 'makes us laugh' (127). She then uses a description of Millett's appearance to reinforce her comparison, describing Millett as:

> short, rather plump, with long brown hair, a particularly soft voice, and an open smile. When I met her at a party to launch her book she was wearing a kaftan and hardly any make up. She did not seem to be enjoying herself, and clearly loathes publicity. She apologised for not granting an interview with *Vouge* ... I would call her [Millett] the movement's bulldozer if the word itself didn't have such a chauvinistic ring. (Tynan 1971, 127)

Throughout the article, Millett and Greer are compared. Greer is positioned as a fashionable, attractive and funny feminist, while Millett is identified as clever, but as lacking humour and style. Crucial to this comparison is Tynan's brief mention of Millett's recent public identification as bisexual. She quotes Greer: 'she [Millett] "paid her dues in the destruction of privacy, in bearing abuse, when she let slip ingeniously that she was (as we all are) bisexual"' (Tynan 1971, 127). Greer's heterosexuality is emphasised throughout by statements such as: 'One girlfriend comments "Germaine can't understand why you should mind if she makes it with your man"' (Tynan 1971, 126). The article subtly connects fashionableness with heterosexuality and humour.

Life magazine makes similar connections to *Vogue*, as Bonfante explicitly connects Greer's heterosexuality with her thoughts on fashion:

> Sensuous and attractive to men, Germaine Greer makes no secret of the fact that she enjoys their company too. "I don't go for the whole pants and battledress routine, it just puts men off and there's already too much defensiveness in the movement". (Bonfante 1971, 30)

Here, Bonfante links heterosexual feminists with fashion, and lesbian feminists with defensive anti-fashion statements. Greer's laughter has a specific place in this arrangement. As part of the publication in *Life*, Greer was presented with 57 photographs from the shoot (excluding the photos printed in the May issue), which are now held by the Greer Archive at the University of Melbourne (Unit 473). She chose to wear the paisley coat for the majority of the photographs. One of the rejected images shows Greer checking out dresses and shopping in New York, another shows her cradling a baby and one has her swirling around and cutely pulling her dress up for the photographer. Several images catch her frowning severely, but none of these are included in *Life's* publication. *Life* deliberately chose to place an image of Greer laughing prominently on the cover. *Vogue* made a similar choice, as they also place an image of Greer laughing in the centre of their feature. Greer is often photographed laughing. As Taylor (2014, 767–69) argues, laughter is one of Greer's media strategies. Laughter makes feminism pleasurable and funny. The presentation of Greer laughing, both in 1971 and now disrupts the stereotype of the humourless feminist (Ahmed 2010, 88; Taylor 2014, 69). However, in the early 1970s, Greer's presentation as funny reiterated the negative representation of Millett and lesbianism circulating in the press, as Greer's sense of humour is presented alongside her heterosexuality. This is best demonstrated by the inclusion of one particular image in *Life*, the full page black and white image of Greer cradling Dick Fontaine. This image explicitly connects heterosexuality and humour, as the photograph shows Greer holding Fontaine and laughing while watching her appearance on American television. *Life* wittily describes the photograph as 'Germaine Greer, giggler, watching Germaine Greer' (Bonfante 1971, 34). This statement functions in the text to reassert the connection already established between heterosexuality, fashion and humour, and reiterates the relationship between anti-fashion statements, humourlessness and lesbianism. Greer's paisley coat became a feminist fashion icon as part of this process, and it is this international historical context that has a ghostly presence when encountering Greer's coat at the National Museum of Australia.

Feminism, fashion and protest

Feminists have primarily remembered the relationship between fashion and women's liberation via protests; the 'No More Miss America!' protest in Atlantic City in 1968 is important when considering this memory. The protest is often remembered as the 'beginning' of women's liberation, as it marked the beginning of a new relationship between feminist protesters and the press, and it has become a symbol of the movement (Luther-Hillman 2013, 157–158; Hesford 2013, 2, 30). The protest is where the stereotype of the 'bra burning' feminist was created and the event has been remembered as a statement against fashion (Groenveld 2009, 181; Luther-Hillman 2013, 157–158). The organisers of The 'No More Miss America!' protest describe their intentions as: 'We will protest the image of Miss America, an image that oppresses women in every area in which it purports to represent us' (Anon [1968] 2010, 90). Organisers of the protest asked women to 'bring any such woman-garbage you have around the house' such as 'bras, girdles, curlers, false eyelashes, wigs, and representative issues of *Cosmopolitan, Ladies Home Journal, Family Circle etc.*' to throw into the 'Freedom Trash Can'. The items thrown in the 'Freedom Trash Can' were never burnt, but the story that feminists burnt their bras endures, as even academic articles still occasionally keep the myth alive (Welters 2008, 499). Although the protest has been memorialised as an anti-fashion statement, to an extent it was an ambivalent one. This ambivalence, and the contested place of the protest in feminist memory, is captured by Henry's (2012, 14) autobiographical reflections:

> Looking at photos from the 1968 Miss America protest, it wasn't just the words on their demonstration signs that caught my eye: Look at those great dresses! That necklace is amazing! I wish I had a pair of sandals like that! These were hip feminists, women who were definitely in on the joke as they paraded a crowned sheep down the Atlantic City boardwalk to 'parody the way the contestants (all women) are appraised and judged like animals at the fair' they were protesting the confines of traditional femininity but they were doing it with flair and with great outfits. I admired them for their style—both in politics and in clothes.

As Henry's implies, feminist protests of fashion in the 1960s and 1970s were embodied, creative and often employed parodies of fashion.

In the late 1960s and early 1970s, feminists developed at least two distinct ways to embody protests of fashion: 'Some feminists argued that it was necessary to reject feminine fashion by adopting masculine dress while others argued that it was necessary to step outside of fashion altogether to reclaim a "natural" female self (Hollows 2000, 140)'. Brownmiller's *Femininity* (1984) is an example of the first approach, while Greer's ([1970] 1971) *The Female Eunuch* is an example of the latter. Brownmiller argued that 'feminine' fashions are central to maintaining differences between men and women, and are part of women's oppression. Brownmiller's (1984, 83–84) solution is to reject dresses, skirts, make up, nylons, stop shaving her legs and reject all forms of 'feminine' dress, because the 'nature of feminine dressing is superficial in essence'. She advocates 'functional' dress: 'Trousers are practical. They cover the lower half of the body without nonsense and permit the freest of natural movements. And therein lies their unfeminine danger'. Brownmiller's *Femininity* sums up one point of view that has circulated in various forms since the late 1960s (Wilson [1986] 2003, 232234; Negrin 2008, 33–38). In comparison, Greer's ([1970] 1971) approach in *The Female Eunuch* is quite different, as she does not insist that women need to give up 'feminine' styles and she has a different definition and vision of 'authenticity'. In *The Female Eunuch*, Greer ([1970] 1971, 58) is critical of fashion and fashion magazines, as she understands them as prescribing femininity and producing a variation of the 'Eternal Feminine'. She argues that fashion (as seasonal change in dress) should be ignored, but she does not reject an interest in styling or modifying according to women's particular bodies. Regarding fashion and dress, Greer (1971, 326) ultimately states that:

> The chief means of liberation is replacing of compulsiveness and compulsion by the pleasure principle. Cooking, clothes, beauty, and housekeeping are all compulsive activities in which the anxiety quotient has long since replaced the pleasure or achievement quotient. It is possible to use even cooking, clothes, cosmetics and housekeeping for *fun*. The essence of pleasure is spontaneity. In these cases spontaneity means rejecting the norm, the standard that one must live up to and establishing a self-regulating system.

Greer's (1971, 58, 325–326) central point is that rather than following 'sexless' fashion models, women can develop their own 'authentic' style based on their (sexual) pleasure, humour and enjoyment, beyond the dictates of the fashion system. Both Brownmiller and Greer's approaches to fashion sit comfortably within the framing provided by the 1968 Miss America protest. Importantly, both are critical of fashion on the grounds that it oppresses women and they propose that women should protest fashion by dressing differently. Developing alternative styles was a creative embodied process, which responded to current fashions. Rather than being outside the fashion system or subservient to it, feminist's protesting fashion through their dress practices unintentionally *created* fashion trends. The dynamic relationship between protesting fashion and creating fashion in the late 1960s and early 1970s is demonstrated by Greer's writing and textile practices.

In her writing, Greer emphasises personal style and uses parody to critique the fashion system. In 'My Mailer Problem', first published in *Esquire* in 1971 Greer (1986, 85–86) mocks the American press's interpretation of her clothes worn during her trip to New York: 'My fox fur, which I had worn for fun and satire because it cost a pound … was so wildly reported as elegance'. In September 1971, in the months after she appeared in *Vogue*, she wrote a short article titled 'Going Without' about underpants, which opens: 'Lately I've been thinking that I was getting rather hip where clothes are concerned. I've finally managed to accumulate some that I like, mostly oldies, but most important they are all comfortable' (1986, 90).[9] In this short article she continues with a story about her gynaecologist's surprise that she sometimes wears knickers. The importance of parody is further demonstrated by Greer's writing about needlework. Under the name of the '*Oz* Needlework Correspondent', Greer published an article that features instructions for embroidering nipples and a 'cunt' motif, and instructions for crocheting 'The Keep it Warm Cock Sock'. The article in *Oz* includes an image of a finished 'bra and pantie set'. Her commentary mocks women's magazines:

> This version was worked on a bra-and-pantie set in Anchor Soft Embroidery cotton. Our photograph shows just one way of using the idea, but apart from sun bathing at the beach or your favourite summer festival, it can be employed to jazz up tired undies, freshen up last year's little black dress, or even provide a focal point on a *grande robe de soir*. Worked in metallic threads and sequins, or even a collage of re-embroidered lace and ribbons, it would be a stunning and enriching motif for that most important of dresses, your bridal gown. (Oz Needlework Correspondent [Greer] 1970, 3)

In *Oz*, Greer uses textiles to parody a particular type of respectable domestic femininity and the fashion system. In the 1970s, feminists often subverted embroidery to make feminist statements (Parker 1984, 205–215).[10] Parker's *The Subversive Stitch* does not specifically discuss dressmaking, but like embroidery, dressmaking is associated with 'traditional' femininity (Burman 2000, 10). When embroidering the 'bra and pantie set' for *Oz* and sewing the paisley coat, Greer is repurposing a feminine skill associated with virtue and the home (Parker 1984, 1–16). She is making a feminist statement that disrupts the presumed relationship between textiles, domesticity and femininity. However, this was not happening 'outside' the fashion system, nor was it subservient to fashion. Instead, in the late 1960s and early 1970s, fashion and feminist protest responded to one another (Davis 1992, 161–188; Steele 1997, 280; Barnard 2002, 127–155).

In the 1960s, various protest movements, including women's liberation, sought to challenge fashion as a concept and rejected the necessity to seasonally update and change dress (Barnard [1996] 2002, 141–155; Welters 2008, 490–500). As well as critiquing the fashion system on socialist, racial or environmental grounds, some feminists specifically argued that fashionable beauty practices oppressed women. People critical of fashion developed alternative styles to the ones featured in fashion magazines, often this involved presenting what was perceived as an 'unfashioned' and 'natural' body (Welters 2008). Women often rejected (or in some cases appeared to reject) underwear, bras, girdles, hair products, curlers, straighteners and make up (Welters 2008, 491–500). This also often involved adopting dress perceived as 'outside' the western fashion system. 'Ethnic' clothes (particularly South Asian dress), antique and vintage clothing from purchased from second hand shops and homemade clothing were all perceived as ways to avoid participating in fashion (Welters 2008, 491–500; Wilson [1986] 2003, 240). By the early 1970s, both the language and style of counter-cultural protest became part of 'fashion' (Wilson [1986] 2003; Steele 1997; Welters 2008) 'Arbiters of fashion' could no longer dictate what was 'in' or 'out' (Steele 1997, 280). Fashion journalists responded to feminist criticism by adopting the language of 'choice' and describing women as having the 'freedom' to choose their own style (Steele 1997, 260, 280; Luther-Hillman 2013,

173–175). Counter-cultural styles were selectively commodified and fashion scholars now call this the 'natural look', which was 'in' from the early to the mid 1970s (Steele 1997; Welters 2008). Evan and Thornton (1989, 13) argue that the natural look still took considerable labour, but rendered that labour invisible.

Greer's coat is an excellent example of the 'natural look'. The NMA speculate that Greer designed the coat by modifying a kaftan pattern.[11] Greer collects textiles; she writes with great joy about her heirloom collection in a short review titled 'I've braved earthquakes and bullets in my hunt for fabulous fabrics' (2010). Fascination with 'ethic' dress has a long history of shaping western fashion. Shawls featuring the teardrop shaped 'paisley' design arrived in Europe from Kashmir in the second half of the eighteenth century. From the late eighteenth century to the 1870s, paisley shawls were an integral part of women's fashion (Rehman and Jafri 2006, 358–360). The paisley pattern, and European interpretations of South Asian dress, became fashionable in the 1960s. In 1964 the bespoke Italian tailor Caraceni was inspired by the first Indian Prime Minister's clothes, and remade a nineteenth century paisley shawl into a 'Nehru' jacket (Martin and Koda 1994, 39). As a garment handmade from a second hand paisley shawl with a design based on South Asian clothing, Greer's coat is representative of late 1960s counter-culture styles, which embodied a protest of fashion. However, by the early 1970s, anti-fashion dress influenced and defined what was 'fashionable' in fashion magazines, and Greer's appearance in *Vogue* and *Life* can be read as a defining part of this trend. Rather than being outside the fashion system or subservient to it, protests against fashion unintentionally created fashion trends. The coat demonstrates the dynamic relationship between protesting fashion and creating fashion in the late 1960s and early 1970s.

Remembering a fashion icon

In 2010, Greer presented her paisley coat and a shawl fragment to the NMA. The intention when collecting Greer's coat was to place it alongside other feminist material, to diversify the representation of the Australian feminist movement at the museum.[12] Since December 2013, the coat and shawl fragment have been on display in a cabinet in the *Journeys: Australia's Connections with the World* gallery (Figures 1 and 2). The *Journeys* gallery places Australia in a transnational context, depicting how people, things and ideas travel to and from Australia. The museum is shaped like a snail's shell, curved around a central courtyard. Within the space, there are five themed exhibition spaces titled: *Journeys, Landmarks, First Australians, Old/New Land* and *Eternity*. Each section presents a particular perspective on Australian history. The *Journeys* gallery is suspended above the other galleries; its shape is vaguely reminiscent of a ship's hull. Its organisation is loosely chronological, with the wall text claiming to move from the 'present' to the 'past', but in practice visitors can enter either side of the exhibition. Greer's coat and shawl fragment is positioned near one end of the gallery, close to the 'present'. It is placed alongside an exhibition about Miss Australia and Miss International winners. The Greer and Miss Australia exhibitions were developed separately, but for audiences aware of the history of feminist protest, this arrangement is highly evocative. Rather than specifically remembering the Australian women's liberation movement, the display of the coat evokes international and specifically Anglo-American feminist memories. The display challenges Greer's place within feminist memory, and challenges how feminists remember women's liberation, fashion and protest.

The NMA present Greer in several ways: as an expatriate, feminist author, dressmaker and as a fashion icon. Given the coat's location in the *Journeys* gallery, the exhibition evokes Greer as an Australian expatriate. The text panel quote's Greer: 'I regard the happiest day of my life as the day I ran away from home. It was a long day, because I didn't stop running til I fetched up in Europe'. The panel foregrounds Greer leaving to take up a Commonwealth scholarship at Cambridge and her brief return to Australia in 1972 to promote *The Female Eunuch*. As well as presenting Greer as an expatriate, the NMA depict her as an important international feminist author. A copy of *The Female Eunuch* (Greer [1970] 1971) and a copy of *Oz* (1970) magazine are located beside the coat. One text panel calls Greer a 'feminist champion', and draws attention to her rise to fame with the publication of *The Female Eunuch* and her feminist celebrity status. The exhibition also presents Greer as a dressmaker as the NMA prominently display the frayed and cut up paisley shawl fragment from which she made the coat. The text also draws attention to her interest in textile collecting and her dressmaking skills. Finally, the exhibition implies that Greer was a fashion icon. A copy of *Life* with Greer on the cover is placed beside the coat. One panel quotes Greer: 'The coat was representative of counterculture style in that period, and of me, I think'. The panel also sketches a brief history of the paisley pattern, its fall from fashion in the late nineteenth century and its 'resurgence as part of counter culture fashions' in the 1960s. The text locates Greer's coat as part of this resurgence. Besides displaying objects associated with Greer, the rest of the cabinet presents dresses, trophies and ephemera from Miss Australia and Miss International competitions (Figures 3–5)

The Miss Australia display prominently includes Tricia Reschke's short white dress with embroidered wattles from 1962, and Tania Verstak's trophy and her bright orange silk chiffon dress from 1961 (Figures 3–5). Verstak was the first naturalised Australian to win the Miss Australia Quest, and also won the US-based Miss International title. Verstak's placement in the *Journeys* gallery highlights her migration experience as well as her participation in the Miss International competition, reflecting shifts in Australian identity and movement in the post-war period. A panel accompanying the display states:

> Each Australian state finalist was judged on 'beauty of face and figure' deportment, diction, personality, social graces and general knowledge .... As a symbol of perfect Australian womanhood and an ambassador for the nation, the much coveted title was traditionally awarded to a middle-class, Anglo-Australian woman. Verstak's win reflected a changing, more tolerant Australia.

The text accompanying the display also narrates Verstak's life as a refugee. She was born in China after her parents fled Russia following the 1917 revolution; they came to Australia with assistance in 1951. The text mentions Verstak's public role as an ambassador, her international travel, charity work and advocacy for refugees. In the context of the *Journeys* gallery, Greer and Verstak's stories are both about the idea of Australia, migration and the experience of leaving home. However, placing 'a feminist champion' beside a Miss Australia winner evokes feminist critiques of fashion and beauty. The memory of the 'No More Miss America!' protest continues to shape how we remember women's liberation, but also how we remember beauty contests. Placing the two exhibitions together could easily reiterate simplistic stereotypes of oppressed beauty queens and angry unattractive bra-burning feminists. Greer's coat and Tania Verstak's dress potentially disrupt these stereotypes; both objects gesture towards alternative narratives as the coat indicates that second wave feminists could dress fashionably and influenced fashion, and Verstak's dress, story and trophy imply that beauty competitions could liberate women.

The 'feminist-as-lesbian figure' has a ghostly presence within the exhibition. In contemporary films, Hesford (2013, 216) argues that: 'the ghost of the feminist-as-lesbian appears … not so much as a historical character but as an un-narratable interruption'. In the exhibition of Greer's coat, Kate Millett specifically and lesbian feminisms generally are an un-narrated presence. *Life* magazine's cover, which is included in the exhibition alongside the coat, and the coat itself gestures towards both these figures without naming them. Merely presenting the coat in its historical context evokes, but does not name, the nexus established in *Life* and *Vogue* magazines between heterosexuality, fashionableness and humour on the one hand, and lesbianism, humourlessness and fashion protests. However, focusing on this historical context makes it possible to name these tensions, which shape memories of women's liberation in the present.

Conclusion

In 2012, Greer's televised comment about Australian Prime Minister Julia Gillard's jacket caused outrage (Q&A, 'Politics and porn in a post-feminist world' March, 2012). Following an analysis of the Prime Minister's political performance, Greer stated: 'What I want her to do is get rid of those bloody jackets!' Tony Jones, the moderator responded: 'She should go to him [Rudd] for political advice and you for fashion advice?' Her response caused serious controversy: 'No, it's not even fashion. They don't fit. Every time she turns around, you've got that strange horizontal crease which means they're cut too narrow in the hips. You've got a big arse, Julia, just get on with it'. As Taylor (2014, 760) argues, on television Greer plays 'the unruly woman' and appears on panel shows 'not simply to reinforce her celebrity but to circulate (and perform) a particular feminism'. In this instance, clothes, bodies and politics are discussed with an irreverent and risky humour. Her approach is consistent with statements in *The Whole Woman* (1999, 141) as Greer argues in her most recent work that clothing is not made for women's bodies, which implies that women must modify themselves to fit both an impossible norm and a standardised set of measures. Furthermore —and something that was not remarked upon in the furore provoked by the remarks—her assessment reflects her knowledge and skill as a dressmaker.

The paisley coat illuminates Greer's complex, often controversial and evolving relationship with fashion. However, Greer's paisley coat disrupts how we tend to locate Greer as a subject and women's liberation as an event, which unsettles feminist memory. As Greer says, 'A woman is not her jacket' (Q&A, 'Mutilation and the Media Generation', 27 August 2012), but the making, wearing and display of Greer's coat challenges simple categorisations of Greer herself, questions the presumed relationship between fashion and protest in the 1970s, and subtly changes how we understand feminism's history. The fashionable feminist figure does not sit easily with received understandings or popular memories of the second wave, a movement more generally associated with a radical rejection of fashion as a tool of the patriarchy, tethered to normative femininity. It is this uneasiness that unsettles feminist storytelling. As Hemmings reminds us, we must remain alert to ways in which particular narratives locate feminist subjects and events (2011, 5). Greer's coat questions the historical relationship of women's liberation with fashionable dress.

Notes

1. For feminist approaches to the archive particularly see: Cvetkovich (2003), Dever, Newman, and Vickery (2009) and Eichhorn (2013).
2. For analysis of Greer's recent comments about high profile public women's dress practices, see the conclusion.
3. Church-Gibson (Bruzzi and Church-Gibson 2013, 7) later revised her position to an extent in the revised edition of this book: 'Thirteen years ago we could write, simply, of 'feminism'. Now, as the penultimate section of this book clearly illustrates, it might be wiser to talk of 'feminisms'; there are conflicting ideas and ideals in an area where previously there was some form of consensus'. A chapter in the revised edition by Radner and Smith (2013, 279) opens up the discussion, as they demonstrate that protesters at the 'No More Miss America!' were dressed in contemporary fashions. They assert that the plurality of dress styles worn at the protest represented 'the times' rather than 'feminism itself' and maintain that 'subsequent developments in feminist thought sought to provide a more unified vision of how the feminist ought to look'. Although this revises the assertion that feminists did not engage with fashion, it still implies that women's liberationists were unified in their critique of fashion.
4. Greer's (Greer 1971) *The Female Eunuch* is often remembered as the origin point for second wave feminism and she is often positioned as representative of women's liberation in the present (Dux and Simic 2008, 3–4; Dux 2010, 9–10; Taylor 2014).
5. See: Lord Snowdon, 'Germaine Greer' (vintage bromide print, 1971, 278 mm×272 mm) NPG P813. http://www.npg.org.uk/collections/search/portrait/mw19244/Germaine-Greer.
6. For analysis of Greer's use of parody see the following section titled 'Feminism, fashion and protest'.
7. For analysis of Greer as a feminist celebrity see: Taylor's (2014), Spongberg (1993) and Lilburn, Magarey, and Sheridan (2000).
8. Hesford only briefly refers to Greer. Millett is the central figure in her study.
9. In 1986, Greer reflects that for her regular newspaper column she interspersed … 'bitter animadversions [about abortion] with frivolous columns about moped riding and going knickerless' (xxv) to entertain her readers and keep her job.
10. The ubiquitous T-shirts and posters advertising the 'ladies sewing circle and terrorist society' using the stylized script of the embroidery sampler are just one example of this trend.
11. NMA, personal communication, 7 May 2015.
12. Australian museums have relatively little relating to women's liberation and the intention when collecting the coat was to diversify how we remember the Australian feminist movement. The NMA commissioned Bartlett and Henderson to produce a report and develop a list of feminist objects the museum could acquire for an exhibition (See: Bartlett and Henderson 2013, 85–94).

Acknowledgements

I would like to thank Alexander Davis for reading early drafts of this manuscript and the anonymous reviewers for their engagement and insight. Thanks to the School of History and International Studies at Flinders University for supporting this research.

Disclosure Statement

No potential conflict of interest was reported by the authors.

References

Anon. [1968] 2010. "No More Miss America!" In *Feminist Theory Reader: Local And Global Perspectives*, edited by Carole R. McCann and Seung-Kyung Kim, 90–91. New York: Routledge.
Ahmed, Sara. 2010. *The Promise of Happiness*. Durham: Duke University Press.
Barnard, Malcolm. (1996) 2002. *Fashion as Communication*. New York: Routledge. Reprint.
Bartlett, Alison, and Margaret Henderson. 2013. "The Australian Women's Movement Goes to the Museum: The 'Cultures Of Australian Feminist Activism, 1970–1990' Project." *Women's Studies International Forum* 37(March–April): 85–94.
Beckingham, Carolyn. 2005. *Is Fashion a Woman's Right?* Brighton: Sussex Academic Press.
Bonfante, Jordan. 1971. "Germaine Greer." *Life*, May 7.
Brownmiller, Susan. 1984. *Femininity*. New York: Lindon Press.
Bruzzi, Stella and Pamela Church-Gibson. 2013. "Introduction: The Changed Fashion Landscape of the New Millennium." In *Fashion Cultures Revisited: Theories, Explorations and Analysis*, edited by Stella Bruzzi and Pamela Church Gibson, 1–8. London: Routledge.
Burman, Barbara. 2000. "Introduction." In *The Cultures of Sewing: Gender, Consumption and Home Dressmaking*, edited by Barbara Burman, 1–18. Oxford: Berg.
Church-Gibson, Pamela. 2000. "Redressing the Balance: Patriarchy, Postmodernism and Feminism." In *Fashion Cultures: Theories, Explorations and Analysis*, edited by Stella Bruzzi and Pamela Church Gibson, 349–362. London: Routledge.
Cvetkovich, Ann. 2003. *An Archive of Feelings: Trauma, Sexuality, and Lesbian Public Cultures*. Durham, NC: Duke University Press.
Davis, Fred. 1992. *Fashion, Culture and Identity*. Chicago: The University of Chicago Press.
Dever, Maryanne, Sally Newman, and Ann Vickery. 2009. *The Intimate Archive: Journeys through Private Papers*. Canberra: National Library of Australia.
Dux, Monica. 2010. "Temple of the Female Eunuch: Germaine Greer Forty Years On." *Kill Your Darlings*, July (2): 9–17.
Dux, Monica, and Zora Simic. 2008. *The Great Feminist Denial*. Carlton: University.
Edwards, Tim. 2011. *Fashion in Focus: Concepts, Practices and Politics*. Abingdon: Routledge.
Eichhorn, Kate. 2013. *The Archival Turn in Feminism: Outrage in Order*. Philadelphia: Temple University Press.
Evan, Caroline, and Minna Thornton. 1989. *Women & Fashion: A New Look*. London: Quartet.
Greer, Germaine. (1970) 1971. *The Female Eunuch*. London: Paladin. Reprint.
Greer, Germaine. 1986. *The Madwoman's Underclothes: Essays and Occational Writings 1968–85*. London: Cavaye Place.
Greer, Germaine. 1999. *The Whole Woman*. London: Doubleday.
Groenveld, Elizabeth. 2009. "'Be A Feminist Or Just Dress Like One': BUST, Fashion And Feminism As Lifestyle." *Journal Of Gender Studies* 18 (2): 179–190.
Hemmings, Clare. 2011. *Why Stories Matter: The Political Grammar of Feminist Theory*. Durham, NC: Duke University Press.
Henry, Astrid. 2012. "Fashioning a Feminist Style, Or, How I Learned to Dress from Reading Feminist Theory." In *Fashion Talks: Undressing the Power of Style*, edited by Shira Tarrant and Marjorie Jollies, 209–225. New York, NY: Suny Press.
Hesford, Victoria. 2013. *Feeling Women's Liberation*. Durham: Duke University Press.
Hollows, Joanne. 2000. *Feminism, Femininity and Popular Culture*. Manchester: Manchester University Press.

Lilburn, Sandra, Susan Magarey, and Susan Sheridan. 2000. "Celebrity Feminism as Synthesis: Germaine Greer, The Female Eunuch and the Australian Print Media." *Continuum* 14 (3): 335–348. doi:10.1080/713657725

Luther-Hillman, Betty. 2013. "'The Clothes I Wear Help Me to Know My Own Power': The Politics of Gender Presentation in the Era of Women's Liberation." *Frontiers: A Journal of Women Studies* 34 (2): 155–185. doi:10.5250/fronjwomestud.34.2.0155

Martin, Richard, and Harold Koda. 1994. *Orientalism: Visions of the East in Western Dress.* New York: The Metropolitan Museum of Art.

Negrin, Llewellyn. 2008. *Appearance and Identity: Fashioning the Body in Postmodernity.* New York: Palgrave Macmillan.

Oz Needlework Correspondent [Germaine Greer]. 1970. *New Ways with Play Clothes. OZ 29: Female Energy/Cuntpower OZ* 29: 3–4. http://ro.uow.edu.au/ozlondon/29.

Parker, Rozsika. 1984. *The Subversive Stitch: Embroidery and the Making of the Feminine.* London: The Women's Press.

Radner, Hilary and Natalie Smith. 2013. "Fashion, Feminism and the Neo-Feminist Ideal: From Coco Chanel to Jennifer Lopez." In *Fashion Cultures Revisited: Theories, Explorations and Analysis*, edited by Stella Bruzzi and Pamela Church Gibson, 275–286. London: Routledge.

Rehman, Sherry, and Naheed Jafri. 2006. *The Kashmiri Shawl: From Jamavar to Paisley.* Ahmedabad: Mapin.

Scott, Linda. 2005. *Fresh Lipstick: Redressing Fashion and Feminism.* New York: Palgrave Macmillan.

Spongberg, M. 1993. "If She's so Great, How Come so Many Pigs Dig Her? Germaine Greer and the Malestream Press." *Women's History Review* 2 (3): 407–419.

Steele, Valerie. 1997. "Anti-Fashion: the 1970s." *Fashion Theory: The Journal of Dress, Body and Culture* 1 (3): 279–296.

Taylor, Anthea. 2014. "Germaine Greer's Adaptable Celebrity." *Feminist Media Studies* 14 (5): 759–774.

Tynan, K. 1971. "Germaine Greer … and Kate Millett." Vouge (UK), May.

Welters, Linda. 2008. "The Natural Look: American Style in the 1970s." *Fashion Theory: The Journal of Dress, Body and Culture* 12 (4): 489–510.

Wilson, Elizabeth. (1986) 2003. *Adorned in Dreams: Fashion and Modernity.* London: I.B. Tauis. Reprint.

The second best bed, or the female unique? Germaine Greer's unlikely championing of love and marriage in *Shakespeare's Wife*

Donald McManus

ABSTRACT

Germaine Greer's remarkable career has obscured her original vocation as a Shakespeare scholar. Her drama criticism stands as a corrective check to the conservative, still male-biased, established word on the popular perception of Shakespeare's legacy. As we perversely celebrate the four-hundredth anniversary of Shakespeare's death, it is instructive to re-visit Greer's contribution to our understanding of what his life and work meant, as well as exploring who best hears his voice today. It would have been an easy thing for Greer to let the world forget her formative years as a Shakespeare scholar, and accept the identity of feminist icon. However, with the publication of *Shakespeare's Wife* (2009) she reasserted her scholarly and critical identity in a profoundly stimulating way, re-focusing the discussion of love and marriage she broached in *The Female Eunuch* back to Shakespeare. The most fascinating element of Greer's biography of Ann Hathaway is her ability to shake us back to the fore play of Shakespeare studies with rigorous historical detail. This article explores the points of harmony and contradiction between Greer's Shakespeare criticism and her oft-quoted views on society, sex, marriage and love.

Although I've never met Germaine Greer we share an unlikely history in that my mentor and dissertation advisor at the University of Michigan, John Russell Brown, was on her committee when she defended her doctoral thesis at Cambridge University in 1967. In preparing this essay my first thought was to contact John and ask him for his insight into the wildly unpredictable and exciting woman he had met when she was a graduate student, nervous about having her thesis passed. Sadly, he passed away in September of 2015 just as I was putting this article together. Isn't that just the way? We try to maintain an objective, scholarly and dispassionate academic mask and then something happens to remind us of the importance of life, death, beauty and love in the work we do. John Brown was an old-school British scholar. He considered women to be delightful appendages to the work of men: 'They are so good at collecting, compartmentalizing and organizing. It is their domestic nature I imagine. So useful in any project don't you think?' I am of course corrupting his memory in my clumsy, comical remembrances of his many outrageous utterances. John exemplified the kind of man of that era who was easily smitten by Greer. He was stimulated by her radical ideas about re-imagining Elizabethan drama. The fact that she packaged herself as a mid-century new woman made her all the more intriguing. John's ingrained Oxonian sexism did not blind him to the cogency of Greer's thought. The fact is that John Russell Brown and Germaine Greer had a lot in common. They were both passionate writers who privileged personal responses over established vocabulary and traditional tropes. This article is written in homage to the unapologetically direct and personal approach that both Greer and Brown championed in their own writing.

The contradiction of Greer as a challenging scholar and social critic on the one hand and an emblem of sexual liberation on the other hand, put her at odds with her fellows in both her initial métier as academic Shakespeare scholar and later incarnation as maverick feminist. In his invective-ridden critique of *Shakespeare's Wife*, Conrad cannot reconcile the Greer of feminist fame with Greer the scholar and sarcastically rages at the 'spinster professor' who needs to paint Shakespeare as a 'virile egomaniac' in order to 'justify emasculating him' (2007). Conrad ends his review by suggesting three alternative choices by Bill Bryson, Peter Ackroyd and Stephen Greenblatt for non-experts to discover the life of Shakespeare. All three are male authors specialising in popular non-fiction. Katherine Scheil has acutely framed the battle over ownership of Shakespeare's legacy as a popular culture turf war in which Greer's position as a public personality serves as a countervailing force to Greenblatt's goal of reaching the 'general public': 'Greenblatt's aim was to use his academic reputation to cross the boundary between high culture Shakespeare and popular culture Shakespeare and extend his influence into the general public' (Scheil 2015, 234). This goal of connecting with the general public conveniently bypasses 40 years of feminist criticism on Shakespeare. The target audience is not scholars and academics. Greer's target audience is also that mainstream, non-specialist readership: the general public.

The many detractors and even some of the positive critics of *Shakespeare's Wife* approach the book as if it is a biography of Ann Hathaway, when its genius lies in its ability to serve as a corrective to the innumerable, ludicrous biographies of Ann's husband William Shakespeare.[1] Greer uses Hathaway as her entry point, exhaustively researching details of women's lives in the sixteenth and seventeenth centuries and debunking the hypothetical propositions of what she describes as 'bardolator-biographers', most pointedly Stephen Greenblatt whose book *Will in the World: How Shakespeare Became Shakespeare* was a Pulitzer Prize finalist and best-seller in 2004. Greer argues that Greenblatt is just the last and loudest in a long line of Shakespeare life-spinners who feel the need to demonstrate that the great man had an unsuccessful, perhaps even tragically bad marriage.

Shakespeare's Wife opens with a convincing account of the obsessive habit historians have displayed of belittling the wives of great men throughout history. About the spouse of the granddaddy of western culture, Socrates, she says: 'If Xanthippe had never existed, Bachelor Dons would have had to invent her' (Greer 2007, 1). She recounts the various examples of male geniuses—Dante, Milton, Bacon, Byron—whose bad marriages are part of their mystique, and argues that there has been a compulsion on the part of historians and biographers to believe that great men must needs have had shrewish or slighted bedfellows: 'Until our own time, history focussed on man the achiever; the higher the achiever the more likely it was that the woman who slept in his bed would be judged unworthy of his company' (Greer 2007, 1). Greer's use of the word bed is particularly evocative because it conjures the image of Ann Hathaway's perceived slight in Shakespeare's will in which she was left his 'second best bed'.

The jumping off point for Greenblatt and his many Ann-hating predecessors is the awkward fact that the 'second best bed with the furniture' was all that was left to Ann Shakespeare in Will's will. Greer deals with the nasty tone of the will, which is undeniably what Peter Quince[2] would describe as a 'hard thing' for anyone defending Ann from those who want to paint her as the despised spouse, by pointing out several of the other omissions of the will, most notably any mention of the poet's manuscripts, drafts, poems and papers—the very things we are most interested in today. Ultimately Greer has Ann meeting with Shakespeare's old colleagues to help publish the first folio, a fantasy which, though charming, has little support.

As Greer points out exhaustively, most biographers have viewed Shakespeare's marriage to Ann Hathaway as a mismatch from the beginning. As Roiphe expressed it: 'The prevailing image of Anne Hathaway is that of an illiterate seductress who beguiled the young Shakespeare, conceived a child and ensnared him in a loveless union' (2008). The mature woman Ann is cast as a harridan who captures the heart of an innocent boy, because she was pregnant and 26 and he was a green lad of 18, barely of legal marriage age in England at the time. Greenblatt's chapter on Will's youthful encounter with Ann in *Will in the World* is titled 'Wooing, Wedding, and Repenting' leaving little doubt as to how he views Shakespeare's youthful union and its legacy on the poet. According to *New York Times* reviewer Kakutami, there seems to be a disturbing correlation between constructing a 'Shakespeare' for a popular audience and offering a pejorative portrayal of Anne Hathaway (2004). In her admittedly periodically polemical biography, Greer argues convincingly that the young Will had much more to gain in the match than Ann did. The fact that he may have written much of his early verse to Ann and sought her as a partner in the contractual and business sense is a radical re-visioning of the standard portrayal of their relationship. The imbalance in the relationship makes complete sense to Greer, both from the perspective of Will as budding poet and as a foundation for a functional marriage in which both parties have work to do and do it independently from each other. Greer provides an alternate reading of Ann as a woman of independent means who chose her young man on his merit and then helped support him and prepare for his retirement as a country gentleman through her work in maintaining the Stratford household for all those years while he was in London producing plays. Though admittedly as much of a fantasy as all the other yarns on the life of Shakespeare, it is in step with Greer's 1970s rhetoric about the potential of a preferable, if less inseparable, union between men and women.

It doesn't matter to Greer whether or not Shakespeare the man was a typical misogynist of his era. Whatever his modern fans may think they know about him, Ann knew Will better and for that reason alone it is worth our energy to consider who she might have been, how she might have helped him, and what kind of marriage they may have had. It isn't necessary for Greer to prove that Shakespeare was any less distinctly male and separate from his wife than Greenblatt does, to also argue that their relationship may have been fruitful for both parties.

It is in keeping with much of Greer's thought that men who acknowledge their separateness from women frequently make the best poets and possibly most useful partners to their women. Throughout Greer's career she has had a strange affinity for male authors that the rest of the world tends to think of as misogynist. She devoted an entire volume of critical biography to the seventeenth century English libertine poet Sir John Wilmot Earl of Rochester in 2000:

> Nowadays few male poets would dare to adopt a female voice, but in the seventeenth century poets as apparently macho as Ben Jonson, who killed a man, did not shrink from speaking as women of women's affairs ... Rochester had no hesitation in writing in a female voice. (Greer 2000, 45)

She has admired and written enthusiastically about Byron and Strindberg paradoxically arguing that these authors, like Wilmot, spoke more effectively in a female voice because they acknowledged the unfathomable distance between the sexes.

There can be no doubting that Greer is an admirer of love poems if not love. The recurring contradictions of all her work explore the tension between a desire to be free from men, the invention of love and the enslavement of marriage, and the equally strong desire to join with men in art-making and love-making, if not love. As recently as 8 March 2015, Greer was quoted by Elle Hunt in the *Guardian* ('Germaine Greer says feminism is ageist ... ') reiterating one of her mantras: 'I'm a liberation feminist, not an equality feminist. Equality is a profoundly conservative aim and it won't achieve anything.' Her consistency in rejecting notions of equality with men has its counterpart with her analysis of poetry and drama. What she has consistently implied in her literary criticism is that the greatest love poems are those that seek to supersede societal restrictions and frankly engage with the differences between men and women, and by doing so envision an erotic universe where men and women might both be greater than the sum of their parts. This might seem a discreet parsing of the opposition of sexual aesthetics that Mailer (1971) and Greer separately propagandised, but her literary research has been preoccupied with the classical, courtly love and Petrarchan roots of most English-language poetry and verse drama. As Greer reminds us in her chapter on how Will may have wooed Ann, the courtly love tradition usually pits a young and socially inferior poet seeking to gain the status of the female object beyond his reach. Far from becoming so liberated that they would no longer need love, much of the argument of second-wave feminism during the 1970s evoked a potential future where marriage could be more successful, and love more attainable if women could gain independence.

Friedan provided a poignantly neo-romantic vision of the couple of the future when she said that the woman who frees herself from *The Feminine Mystique*:

> will not need the regard of boy or man to feel alive. And when women do not need to live through their husbands and children, men will not fear the love and strength of women, nor need another's weakness to prove their own masculinity. (1963, 377–8)

It is fair to say that Greer's reading of Shakespeare discovers Friedan's rhapsodic vision of the future embedded in the literary heritage of the past.

Lists of Greer's published works foreground her social criticism and obfuscate her considerable output as an analyst of literature, poetry, drama and art. Her status as a feminist iconoclast has so overshadowed her métier as a literary critic that in a recent foray into the electronic search system *Artemis*, presumably named after the Goddess of the hunt, but seemingly dedicated to seeking and avoiding, I entered Greer's name and the word Shakespeare did not even appear. It would appear that an entire generation of Google-driven undergraduate students are using research tools that obscure Greer's identity as a scholar. And yet her career began at Cambridge with a Doctoral thesis entitled 'The Ethic of Love and Marriage in Shakespeare's Early Comedies'.

It is endlessly fascinating to compare and contrast Greer's literary criticism with her social criticism. The extent to which the one supports and at times contradicts the other enlightens both aspects of her identity and the workings of her mind. If she paints a picture of, if not a more perfect marriage at least a less horrible one than past biographers of Will and Ann, does such a vision distort or contradict her apparent loathing of marriage and even monogamy expressed elsewhere? Is she less of a feminist, or at any rate a different kind of feminist, when reading Shakespeare?

I am probably a good example of what Greer described as that peculiarly American phenomenon of 'a breed of men who claim to be feminists' (1986a, 207). These men try to envision equality and coexistence with women, in contradistinction to some of Greer's literary heroes who acknowledged what she describes as the 'eternal war' (1986a, 207). If I am like the men Greer satirises in this quote she is to blame, because I read *The Female Eunuch* when I was around 12 or 13 years old. Re-reading that book in preparation for this essay I was struck by how graphic it was especially regarding sex and power:

> Every time women have been given a gun for the duration of a specific struggle, it has been withdrawn and they have found themselves more impotent than before. The process to be followed is the opposite: women must humanize the penis, take the steel out of it and make it flesh again. (Greer 1970, 315)

As Greer was to say many years later in *The Whole Woman* 'What red-blooded male would settle for being a nice boy when he could as easily become a love rat or a shag monster?' (1999, 329) So how does Greer's reading of Shakespeare accord with her other statements concerning men and women, marriage and sexual understanding?

Greer says she grew up with few books in her house, but one of them was Shakespeare's complete works. She claims not to have thought much about Shakespeare's actual life until later in her career when she was forced to compile a bibliography of Shakespeare biography for students:

> I was appalled. Appalled by the sheer perversity of what my distinguished colleagues chose to believe about Shakespeare. Part of what they believed was that Shakespeare abandoned his wife and children in 1585, or thereabouts, and then moved back into the marital home after twenty-six years or so of bachelor living in London. (Greer 2013)

It is clear from this anecdote that whatever it was that drew her to Shakespeare originally, her impulse to write about Ann Hathaway was directly connected to her outrage at the male-dominated structure of academe. At the forefront of that outrage is the repetition of received ideas that pass for scholarship in most biographies. She had already made this point in her book on Wilmot, the opening chapter of which is almost entirely devoted to debunking the received wisdom of Wilmot as 'Rake Rochester' and complaining about 'the mass of inaccuracy, distortion and downright error that obscures the life and work of Rochester' (Greer 2000, 8). Where her trashing of the centuries of erroneous, rumour-driven biographies of Wilmot is impressive, hardly anyone outside of academic literary studies actually cares about, or has in all honesty even heard of *John Wilmot, Earl of Rochester*, whereas almost everyone has an opinion about William Shakespeare of Stratford upon Avon, glover's son.

The speculations that Greer presents in *Shakespeare's Wife* are another chapter in Shakespearean fantasy biography, and like the vast majority of Shakespeare biographies reflect the biases of their author. But Greer's vision disturbs the traditional, received narrative of Shakespeare's life, marriage and idea of woman in an entirely positive way. Her argument gives modern readers a fresh way of engaging with the plays that avoids the new historicist tendency of reading Shakespeare as a product of his time, who, while a genius, was a mouthpiece for Renaissance values that are ultimately foreign and irrelevant to our time and culture. Scheil specifically contrasts Greer's strategy with the new historicism suggesting that:

> Empowering Ann Hathaway through association with a modern paradigm for women's lives that contemporary audiences can relate to (such as a work-at-home mother or stay-at-home mother) also has the effect of giving value to her domestic life, in line with the many recent revisionist works on the history of domesticity. (2015, 235)

As Scheil implies, Greer's reading of the Shakespeare marriage is designed to bring the past into the present by connecting it with domestic problems that continue to haunt us. Most remarkably, however, Greer also seems to contradict some of her own, more polemical, statements regarding monogamy, marriage and sex in her earlier writings. Looking back at where she entered the field and where we have come to now, one can only marvel that she continues to prompt us all to think differently, beginning I suggest, with a reevaluation of her own ideas.

It is undeniable that her penchant for hyperbole comes back to haunt her. Greer wrote in 1972 that she found 'monogamy the most incomprehensible perversion of all' (quoted in 1986a, 102). The apparently irreconcilable contradictions between love, marriage, liberation, child-rearing and sexual longing permeate all of Greer's work, but the tension between her suspicion of love, marriage and monogamy and an alternative vision for how these ideals can be lived in the real world is more present in *Shakespeare's Wife* than in any of Greer's other writings.

The same author who wrote of 'The Middle-Class Myth of Love and Marriage' in *The Female Eunuch* seems to defend love and marriage in *Shakespeare's Wife*:

> If Ann loved Will, and we shall decide in default of evidence to the contrary that she did, she must have missed him terribly, especially in the long dark winter evenings, when she sat working by the dying fire as her children slept. (Greer 2007, 147)

In default of evidence to the contrary we should assume that love existed even though Greer elsewhere claimed that monogamy was perverse, even biologically unsound. Chapter 19 of *Shakespeare's Wife* considers the problematic will in which Will left Ann his 'second best bed'. Greer takes this most problematic piece of anti-Ann evidence and deconstructs the problems of the estate, arguing convincingly that the will has many similar more egregious omissions and flaws and concluding with the unambiguously romantic suggestion: 'If we assume that Ann had her widow's coffer to go along with her widow-bed, her future begins to look rather more interesting, worthier of

Shakespeare's oldest, truest love' (2007, 325). It is as if her defense of Ann from other Shakespeare biographers prompts her to reevaluate marriage and love in a positive light. It could be that she romanticises this specific marriage because Shakespeare is such an important playwright and cultural figure, but she extends her marriage-positive rhetoric to the disinherited younger daughter Judith whose relationship with her husband, the publican at Stratford's 'The Cage' she says:

> … the marriage seems to have been a real one. Thomas might have been unreliable and impractical but he might also have been fun. While Susanna busied herself in her huge house with her one daughter, living the life of a gentlewoman, Judith and Thomas seem to have lived at the Cage like lovers. (Greer 2007, 329)

Greer implies that some marriages are 'real' while others are not and furthermore that living 'like lovers' is symptomatic of real marriage.

As has already been suggested, her main goal was to react to the assault on Ann Hathaway by Stephen Greenblatt in his gratuitously praised, outrageously hypothetical biography of Shakespeare *Will in the World*. Is Greer circling the wagons to defend the poet's woman against a sea of hostility, and in doing so reverse her hyperbolic antagonism toward love, monogamy and matrimony? The answer to this question is almost certainly yes. She is not alone in pointing out the tale-spinning flaws of *Will in the World*: 'Almost every step forward in reconstructing his life involves a step backward into conjecture and a further step sometimes into pure foolishness' (Toibin 2004). *Shakespeare's Wife* has been criticised for the same whimsical storytelling, or according to the acerbic Conrad, being more hearsay than heresy (2007). But the whole point of her book is to provide alternative possibilities to accepted histories.

Greer has always been a reactive critic. By that I mean that she responds to the outrageous cultural clutter around her with invective, and wit. It is also true that her most outrageous sound bites have been repeated over and over again without the reactive context that prompted them. A close reading of her criticism from the beginning of her career illuminates what might appear as a reversal in her twenty-first century position on marriage. Ultimately, her contradictions are the core of her consistency.

Greer's doctoral thesis, 'The Ethic of Love and Marriage in Shakespeare's Early Comedies', completed at Cambridge University in 1967, offers an important glimpse into her pre-celebrity-pundit mind. The most striking aspect of the thesis is that her approach to Shakespeare was iconoclastic from the beginning. Examining how she thinks as a literary scholar provides texture and context to her public position as feminist commentator. Of particular interest is her focus on love, sex and marriage in the formative years of Shakespeare's creative life. She argues that the early plays reveal the experimental nature of his artistry and that it was both socially and dramaturgically revolutionary. Even the contradictions that can be found between her thesis and *The Female Eunuch* written less than five years later, developed somewhat in *Shakespeare* (1986b) and expanded in *Shakespeare's Wife* three decades later, constitute a consistent critical apparatus. It could be argued that a way of understanding Greer's broader critical thinking is to listen to what she says about Shakespeare's enduring appeal.

In her doctoral thesis her primary idea is that Shakespeare is an experimental artist comparable to modern-day, or at least twentieth century avant-gardists who challenge conventions in sometimes aggressive ways. More traditionally, she spends a lot of energy placing these experiments in the context of late Renaissance, continental models. What from the Spanish and Italian masters did Shakespeare select and refine? How did he adopt and reject what came before? Even experimenters choose a path to follow or reject and are influenced by what has come before:

> Machiavelli represents the half-way mark, for underneath the story of sly conveyance of whoredom flows the vitriolic stream of his satiric conscience. For Shakespeare the choice was open, either the old moralized classicism, or the scurrilous comedy of the satirists, or a rejection of all learned prescriptions for the living aesthetic of the theatre itself. (Greer 1967, 8)

Interestingly her answer to this implied question is seated in the activity of playing for the Elizabethan audience. Greer suggests that the relationship between the poet and his audience helped him shape his art in a new and dynamic direction: 'The story of the greatness of Elizabethan theatre is also the story of the greatness of the Elizabethan audience, with its strong admixture of farmers and poor country hinds' (1967, 10). It is important to point out that Greer's celebration of the audience as a co-author of Shakespeare's aesthetics, as implied by the above quotation from her thesis, is unusual. It is an idea she repeated even more elegantly in her book *Shakespeare*: 'Indeed, it might be said that the strength of Shakespeare's position is that he refrains from coming to conclusions but leaves that to those who complete his utterance, the audience and the actors in the theatre' (Greer 1986b, 40). Greer's vision of the audience implies a kind of Utopian, democratic faith in the discursive contribution of the common, undocumented and forgotten folk of history. Women are of course much more likely to be forgotten than men, even when they are the marriage partner to the world's greatest playwright. Germaine Greer made it her mission to demand that we acknowledge the contributions of forgotten women and men even if that involves sifting endless palimpsests of obscured documents for the trace of these erased souls. *Shakespeare's Wife* is less about Ann Hathaway, the invisible partner of the great playwright, than it is about all the similarly stationed women and men whose contributions to the greatest moments of history have been perniciously obscured. She devotes much of the book to describing the work of women who earned their living in the period as haberdashers, brewers, basket makers, farmers, small loan bankers, silk makers, etc. to suggest that Ann could have shared that life and been independent through her labour. The fact that there is no direct evidence for Ann being connected to this labour is irrelevant. It is the ignored historical evidence of women's work that is important.

Most criticism of Germaine Greer characterises her as a prescriptive and proscriptive social commentator urging women and men to follow her lead. Wallace makes this reading of Greer unambiguous when she confronts her unapologetic heterosexuality by saying that *The Female Eunuch* did not:

> allow for the possibility that a lesbian could be liberated, for example, or that a celibate woman could be liberated, or that a woman content with self-pleasuring could be liberated. In this respect *The Female Eunuch* is one of the prescriptive extremes of second-wave feminism, every bit as wrong headed as the other extreme dictating that only lesbians could consider themselves true feminists. (1998, 164)

Conspicuously missing in Wallace's catalogue of marginalised potential members of the sisterhood of the liberated are married women in monogamous relationships. Marriage and monogamy are the primary targets in *Eunuch*, not self-pleasuring and lesbianism. However accurate and supportable Wallace's criticism may be for the heteronormative bias of *Eunuch*, Greer's championing of the Renaissance audience as a cultural force gives the lie to the oft repeated generalisation that Greer is 'prescriptive'. Despite multiple examples where Greer states clearly that she was not telling any women how to behave, it is her more hyperbolic utterances, which seemed to be promoting extreme behaviour, that have received the most press and shaped her popular persona:

> The fact that I am a law-breaker does not entail the notion that I must be a law-maker. Because I ran away from my own husband and find monogamy the most incomprehensible perversion of all, I am wrongly assumed to order all other women into a life of promiscuity. Because I do not wear a brassiere and do not believe that women ought to feel obliged to wear such an unbecoming garment, it is said that I have ordered all women to throw away such underwear, to burn it even. (Greer 1986a, 102)

Sometimes perception trumps evidence.

Although it escaped a lot of attention in the media frenzy that followed the release of *The Female Eunuch*, Greer included quite a bit of Shakespeare analysis in that book. She recycles some of the key ideas from her doctoral thesis in the chapter titled 'The Middle-Class Myth of Love and Marriage'. This chapter argues that the concepts of love and marriage were developed and adapted over several centuries into a dysfunctional myth system that frustrated the desires and aspirations of both husbands and wives in the modern era. The revolution that is called for in the final chapter of *The Female Eunuch* is predicated on women and men overcoming together the inherited ignorance of the history of religious, political and literary influences that had conspired to create this myth. Central to the argument is the section that deals with the English Renaissance: 'One of the most significant apologists of marriage as a way of life and road to salvation was Shakespeare' (Greer 1970, 204). In this phrase she sounds like an anti-Shakespearean targeting his status in the inherited literary culture as a primary device to sell marriage as the most effective way of controlling female sexuality and competition. Such an argument would echo her anti-monogamous and anti-matrimonial statements elsewhere in *The Female Eunuch*. But she goes on to say that:

> one thing is clear—that he was as much concerned in his new fangled comedies to clear away the detritus of romance, ritual, perversity and obsession as he was to achieve happy endings, and many of the difficulties in his plays are resolved when we can discern this principle at work. (Greer 1970, 204)

This contextualising implies that Shakespeare envisages a different kind of union, marriage, or mode of playing out relationships.

She analyses the effectiveness, and one might say, modernity of Shakespeare's heroines claiming that 'when the choice lies between the ultra-feminine and the virago, Shakespeare's sympathy lies with the virago' (Greer 1970, 204). Much like the later feminist theatre critic Sue Ellen Case, she resists opting for a formula where the heroines of comedy are positive and the heroines of tragedy are negative, but unlike Case she gives much more control and power to the women in the audience watching these remarkable fictional women being portrayed by so-called boy actors. Case argues that a feminist interpretation of Shakespeare's theatre has to begin with the essentially misogynist nature of boy actors playing all the women.

Where Case sees love play between boy actors playing women and male actors playing men as a joke on the women in the audience, Greer sees the un-segregated audience as active players: 'The notion of egalitarian marriage was far from universal in Shakespeare's day, especially among the literate classes' (1986b, 111). Greer implies here an inequality based on class division that is unlike other class inequalities we are used to. Here, the division is imbalanced toward the lower end. But this is logical if we consider that Greer the Marxist is always somewhere in the background guiding Greer the feminist. Marxism was starting to recede as a relevant critical flash point precisely at the time that Greer received her doctorate and announced herself on the public scene as a feminist, but Marxist ideas of a more positive, pre-capitalist domestic life inform much of her thinking. The concept of marriage and concomitant notion of love that Greer challenges in her work is a specific phenomenon that grew out of a more urbanised society and capitalist system. It isn't that Greer is saying that marriage and love are purely constructed, but that they are, like beauty, human longings that have been appropriated, adapted and perverted by a commercial system. There may be a hint of Bakhtin evident when Greer, wanting to avoid a hierarchical and dictatorial misreading of her call for revolution, declares: 'The surest guide to the correctness of the path that women take is *joy in the struggle*. Revolution is the festival of the oppressed' (1970, 328). This promoting of the pleasure principle as a guide to sexual revolution is repeated in her analysis of comedy.

One of the most problematic examples of Greer's promotion of alternatives to conventional marriage in Shakespeare's comedies is her reading of *The Taming of the Shrew* as a radically experimental play. In *The Female Eunuch* she describes Petruchio's taming of Kate in *The Taming of the Shrew* as 'the greatest defense of Christian monogamy ever written' (1970, 207), and she doesn't mean that in an ironic way. The contradictions in Greer's work, especially when one considers her entire output over 40 years, are easy enough to identify. It is tempting to go point by point and identify contradictions; Christine Wallace has done exactly that in her biography of Greer. Wallace is so taken with the absurdity of a feminist extolling the virtues of Shakespeare's most notoriously misogynist comedy, an entire chapter of the doctoral thesis is devoted to *Shrew*, that she calculatedly titled her biography *The Untamed Shrew* in its honour (1998). Paglia subsequently defended Greer from Wallace's critique:

> Greer's thesis, on love and marriage in Shakespeare's early comedies, is distorted by a hostile Wallace, who can't reconcile Greer's real-life 'sexual braggadocio' with the male conquest in *The Taming of the Shrew*—when in fact Greer was asking searching questions about virility and female desire that feminism still cannot answer. (1999)

Whether Paglia's defense of Greer is accurate or not, Wallace missed, or avoids, the central point of Greer's reading of *Shrew*, which is that the play's primary target is the hypocritical, assumed imbalance of the marriage of the sister Bianca. Normative marriage is what is critiqued for its taming of women in *Shrew*, while Kate and Petruchio are, in Greer's mind, a more revolutionary couple because they break all the rules. One could assume Greer's defense of *Shrew* in her thesis was an early anomaly, but she didn't shy away from her Cambridge analysis in her later work. On the contrary, she stated it even more forcefully in *Eunuch*: 'The message is probably twofold: only Kates make good wives and only to Petruchios; for the rest their cake is dough' (Greer 1970, 206). There is an interesting echo of Greer's surprising championing of *Shrew* in her vision of love and marriage in Shakespeare's

Wife, especially the already mentioned characterisation of Judith's 'real marriage' in her husband's pub The Cage where the two lived as 'lovers'.

If we consider her unpublished thesis as her first major statement on Shakespeare and her brief but incisive chapter from *The Female Eunuch* as a dynamic second thrust, her other most important publication on Shakespeare's artistry during the twentieth century, entitled simply *Shakespeare*, seems a slim volume and most notably, disconnected from her feminist social commentary. She actually argues that Shakespeare's lack of coherent social philosophy, a flaw that Tolstoy (1906) and Shaw (1908) both complain about, is the core of his enduring interest:

> The Chief pitfall threatening any discussion of Shakespeare's thought is the common assumption that the opinions of any character in a Shakespeare play are Shakespeare's own. Shakespeare was not a propagandist; he did not write plays as vehicles for his own ideas. Rather he developed a theatre of dialectical conflict, in which idea is pitted against idea and from their friction a deeper understanding of the issues emerges. (Greer 1986b, 17–18)

Only the rarest analysts in the long history of Shakespeare criticism have captured the essence of his dramaturgy in a more succinct and scintillating few words. Greer implies that it is in the interplay between audience and performers that the significance of a work emerges in any given generation. But beyond that empowered vision of the audience is an equally revolutionary empowerment of the social strata that comprised the audience: 'As a playwright, he disciplined his imagination and sang for all men to hear, but especially for the Grumios, Launces, and Costards of the world, whose language was their only patrimony, and their songs their only riches' (Greer 1967, 317). So in Greer's estimation it was the clowns and servants (Grumio, Launce and Costard), the theatrical emblems of rural peasantry hearkening back to a pre-urban, more naturally egalitarian Britain who were the ideal audience for Shakespeare's verse plays. I believe that there is an echo of this sentiment in her final paragraph of *The Whole Woman*:

> The ideological battles that feminist theorists are engaged in are necessary, but they are preliminary to the emergence of female power, which will not flow decorously out from the universities or from the consumerist woman's press. Female power will rush upon us in the persons of women who have nothing to lose, having lot everything already. (Greer 1999, 343)

Greer suggests a tacit solidarity between the women who will manifest 'female power', those un-tenured workers, and Shakespeare's clowns (Grumio, Launce and Costard), the plebeian brothers of the un-named female revolutionaries. Seen in this way, Greer's meticulous recounting of Renaissance midwifery and domestic chores as well as marketable skills that Ann may have used to sustain her family in *Shakespeare's Wife* become consistent with the revolutionary vision that permeates all of Greer's writing.

One of the most powerful and revealing lines in *Shakespeare's Wife* is the first sentence from the introduction: 'Anyone steeped in western literary culture must wonder why any woman of spirit would want to be a wife' (Greer 2007, 1). Literature advertises marriage and the type of marriage it promotes is not to Greer's taste, but does this preclude all notions of love and partnership between men and women? After spending half of *Shakespeare's Wife* convincing readers that the union of Will and Ann could have been something other than a disaster for Shakespeare, Greer goes on to paint an almost romantic vision of Ann's possible management of the family and business in Stratford. She challenges the idea that Will was an absentee husband in any larger sense than any other professional might need to be: 'It is possible of course that Shakespeare never really left Stratford'. Aubrey stated confidently that 'Mr. William Shakespeare was wont to go into Warwickshire once a year ... ' (Greer 2007, 278).[3] Her trump card is the fact that Shakespeare returned to Stratford in his later years. If he had a mistress in London, why not live with her? She points out that Will did not seem to have permanent lodgings in London at any point in his career, choosing rather to rent rooms, suggesting that he was in the city to work and considered his home back in the country with Ann. Shakespeare's lifestyle was not unusual then or now. There have always been men whose careers have taken them away from home for long periods of time for seasonal employment: merchants, seamen, soldiers, etc., and still maintained a home and family. Having a partner to look after their holdings was of course an asset. Greer argues that Shakespeare's retirement to Stratford would never have been possible without her planning for that over the long years of their intermittent separation.

Although Greer elsewhere calls monogamy perverse, she argues that there is no evidence for Will having a mistress or male lover, implying that if Will lacked a lover he must have had a functioning relationship with Ann. But her narrative takes a strange turn by necessarily confronting the possibility that Will would have had relationships with other women and possibly had contact with prostitutes. Resorting to uncharacteristic censoriousness she declares that if Shakespeare 'had gone here and there, defiling his body and compromising his compact with Ann', he was a fool (Greer 2007, 310). The strengths of her book are almost always those sections in which her fantasy is of a working, healthy partnership between Ann and Will. When she considers that Will might have cavorted, her tone becomes personally defensive and outraged. *Shakespeare's Wife* is for the most part the exact opposite of what Conrad says it is when he claims that Greer chose to paint Ann as 'a martyr to her brutish, sadistic husband—in order to satisfy her own grudge against men' (2007). Her strategy is more akin to that of British playwright Edward Bond who said of his fictional/biographical play *Bingo* (1973): 'My account rather flatters Shakespeare. If he didn't end in the way shown in the play, then he was a reactionary blimp or some other fool' (Bond 1975, x).

The weakest section of *Shakespeare's Wife*, which has been pounced on by hostile critics, is where she implies that the doggerel on Shakespeare's grave 'Blest be the man that spares these stones/ And curst be he that moves my bones' is there because his son-in-law John Hall, who was a doctor, stage managed the resting place so that future generations would not examine the bones and reveal that the great man died of syphilis. Despite Conrad's defense of his perceived assault by Greer on biographers who are 'possessors of those opprobrious and lesion-ridden penises', (2007) Greer does not confine her critique of Shakespeare Wallahs exclusively to male biographers. She also satirises the scholarship of Catherine Duncan-Jones: 'She believes that Shakespeare was morbidly obese ... Having created her Falstaffian Shakespeare, Duncan-Jones then turns him into a drunk' (Greer 2007, 295). Why does she allow her argument to transform to the extent that at the beginning of a chapter she is defending 'the Bard's' morals and Ann's honour, and by the end he is dying from over-indulging in whoredom? Greer wants to counter Greenblatt's assertion that the bad poetry on the great poet's tomb is meant to prevent Ann from being buried next to him. In defending Ann from Greenblatt's insistence that Will hated Ann, Greer drifts into the hyperbolic myth-making that most of her book, the best parts of her book, challenge and ridicule.

Although her many side steps into hyperbole obscured her more compelling point even while they propelled her fame, Greer's reading of literature at the twilight of her career seems in step with what she had promoted earlier as a social critic. Her analysis of the genius of Shakespeare's dramatic works reminds us of her Marxist roots, her suspicion of commercialism, her ultimate faith in the power of un-heralded women to come. About Shakespeare she said: 'He was not a propagandist and he did not write plays as vehicles for his own ideas' (Greer 1986b, 17). Similarly Greer's life's work, despite its apparent sound and fury, was neither prescriptive nor proscriptive, but rather, organic, physical, and sensual; as any good performance should be. Indeed she was waiting, and still is I think, for the revolution to come:

> The Second wave of feminism, rather than having crashed on to the shore, is still far out to sea, slowly and inexorably gathering momentum. None of us who are alive today will witness more than the first rumbles of the coming social upheaval. (Greer 1999, 343)

There is a resonance between Greer's vision of a revolutionary upheaval of the future and the revolutionary possibilities reflected in Shakespeare's plays on the one hand, and the courageous efforts to alter the power structure in the early modern era. *Shakespeare's Wife* recounts the social upheaval of the struggle of the landless classes against enclosures that at times broke out into full scale revolution at the exact time that Shakespeare's daughter Susannah was getting married and the poet was setting up house as a country gentleman in Stratford.

Shakespeare's Wife might seem a digression or even reversal to some, but to me it reads as an extension of Greer's earlier revolutionary rhetoric, if distempered with the un-sober second thought in which the desire for a union with that perfect soul, that poet boy from an epoch long lost could merge in some kind of other-worldly unconsidered future with a vibrant female voice from today or tomorrow and finally form that unwanted, perfect pair that so many comedies crave and tragedies lament. Given the consistencies embedded within the many contradictions of her career it may be that Germaine Greer's championing of marriage in *Shakespeare's Wife* is less 'unlikely' than the title of this essay might seem to suggest. By combining a respect for the audience, with a popular feminist response to conservative popular biographies and a sensitivity to the potential of genuine revolutionary change that early modern English culture promised, her re-fashioning of standard Shakespeare and/or Hathaway biography is as exciting, challenging, amusing and confusing as her best work.

Notes

1. I have used 'Ann' throughout this article because that is Greer's preferred spelling.
2. in *A Midsummer Night's Dream* III, I, 861.
3. John Aubrey 1626–1697 was an amateur biographer in the era just following Shakespeare's lifetime.

References

Bond, Edward. 1975. *Bingo*. New York: Hill & Wang.
Conrad, Peter. 2007. "Dr. Greer on the Warpath." *The Guardian*, Sunday September 2.
Friedan, Betty. 1963. *The Feminine Mystique*. New York: W.W. Norton.
Greenblatt, Stephen. 2004. *Will in the World: How Shakespeare Became Shakespeare*. New York: W.W. Norton.
Greer, Germaine. 1967. "The Ethic of Love and Marriage in Shakespeare's Early Comedies." PhD thesis, Cambridge University.
Greer, Germaine. 1970. *The Female Eunuch*. New York: McGraw-Hill.
Greer, Germaine. 1986a. *The Madwoman's Underclothes: Essays and Occasional Writings*. New York: Atlantic Monthly Press.
Greer, Germaine. 1986b. *Shakespeare*. Oxford: Oxford University Press.
Greer, Germaine. 1999. *The Whole Woman*. New York: Alfred A. Knopf.
Greer, Germaine. 2000. *John Wilmot, Earl of Rochester*. Horndon: Northcote House.
Greer, Germaine. 2007. *Shakespeare's Wife*. London: Bloomsbury.
Greer, Germaine. 2013. "Did Shakespeare Love the Cruellest Month?" *The New Yorker*, April 11.
Kakutami, Michiko. 2004. "Shakespeare Attracts a New Pursuer." *New York Times*, October 1.
Mailer, Norman. 1971. *The Prisoner of Sex*. Boston: Little, Brown.
Paglia, Camille. 1999. "Back to the Barricades." *The New York Times* May 9.
Roiphe, Katie. 2008. "Reclaiming the Shrew." *The New York Times*, Sunday Book Review April 27.
Scheil, Katherine. 2015. "Filling in the 'Wife-Shaped Void': The Contemporary Afterlife of Anne Hathaway." *Shakespeare Survey 63* Cambridge University Press, 225–236.
Shaw, Bernard. 1908. "Shakespeare and Shaw." *The Sewanee Review* 16 (2): 169.
Toibin, Colm. 2004. "Will in the World: Reinventing Shakespeare." *The New York Times*, Sunday Book Review, October 3.
Tolstoy, Leo. 1906. *Tolstoy on Shakespeare*. Translated by V. Tchertkoff. New York: Funk & Wagnalls.
Wallace, Christine. 1998. *Germaine Greer: The Untamed Shrew*. New York: Faber&Faber.

Index

Note: page numbers with 'n' denote notes section.

Ackroyd, Peter 96
Adler, Dina 18
The Advertiser 53, 54, 59n5
The Age 54–6
Allegory of the Black Eunuchs (Cleaver) 14, 17
The American Dream (Mailer) 15
Amis, Martin 64
Anderson, John 33, 67
Anderson, Mitzi 67
Arndt, Bettina 35
Aubrey, John 106, 107n3
Australia: Greer's immense contribution in 1; Stassinopoulos, Arianna visited 48–50
Australian Feminist Studies 4
The Australian Women's Weekly 45, 49, 51, 54, 56
Autobiography of Malcolm 12

Baldwin, James 15
Barrett, Jeanne C. 69, 70
Beer, Goldie 72
Benson, Harry 25
Beyond Feminist Aesthetics (Felski) 39
Black Panther Party 12
Bond, Edward 106
Bonfante, Jordan 84, 85
Bongiorno, Frank 11
Borges, Victor 67
Bouton, Jim 68, 70, 71
Box Hill collective 25
Brick, Pam 74n2
Brown, John Russell 95, 96
Brownmiller, Susan 87
Bryson, Bill 96
Bulbeck, Chilla 36

Callil, Carmen 23
Campbell, Beatrix 30
Carmichael, Stokely 29, 40n2
Cavett, Dick 63, 67, 71, 73
Church-Gibson, Pamela 78–81, 83, 92n3
Cleaver, Eldridge 11–15, 17
Cleo magazine 36, 40, 45, 48, 53, 56
clitoral orgasm 29; sexual normativity of 32
Communist Party of Australia 25
Conrad, Peter 96, 106
consciousness-raising techniques 32
Coote, Anna 30
Cosmopolitan magazine 40
The Courier-Mail 51, 53–5
cuntpower theory 2, 33–5; clitoral orgasm and 29; feminist orgasm 31–2; overview of 28–9; Push discussions 33

D'Acci, Julie 75n3
Daly, Jackie 71
Damminger, Jamie 72
Damned Whores and God's Police (Summers) 17
Deacon, Desley 18
Dean, Katrina 3, 23, 26n5
Dean, Tacita 24
de Beauvoir, Simone 12, 13, 17, 18, 23
The Dialectic of Sex (Firestone) 12
Dimen, Muriel 32
DO IT! Scenarios of the Revolution (Greer) 9
Douglas, Susan 72
Dow, Bonnie J. 67
Dreifus, Claudia 66
Ducks on the Pond (Summers) 37
Duncan-Jones, Catherine 106

Echols, Alice 32
Eichhorn, Kate 2, 64
Engelhardt, Molly 64
Eros and Civilisation (Marcuse) 33
Esquire 87
The Ethic of Love and Marriage in Shakespeare's Early Comedies (Greer) 101

Faust, Beatrice 36–7
Fell, Liz 32
Felski, Rita 39

INDEX

The Female Eunuch (Greer) 1, 28, 33–7, 44, 53, 64, 100; *see also* transatlantic orientation
The Female Woman (Stassinopoulos) 43–5, 49; media coverage of 50–3; misrepresenting Greer and women's liberation in 45–8
The Feminine Mystique (Friedan) 12, 98
Femininity (Brownmiller) 87
feminist fashion icon, paisley coat: fashion and women's liberation 86; protesting *vs.* creating fashion 87, 88; in *Vogue* and *Life* magazines 83–6; women's magazines 88
feminist materialist approach 83
feminist orgasm 31–2
Ferguson, Rosetta 67, 68
Festival of Light (FoL) 59n9, 59n10
Firestone, Shulamith 12
Fontaine, Dick 84, 86
Foote, Timothy 65
The Formative Years (de Beauvoir) 17
Forum magazine 34, 35, 39
Freeman, Jo 47
Friedan, Betty 8, 23, 67

Gallop, Jane 29–30
Gemmel, Judy 53
Gerhard, Jane 31
Gibson, Ralph 25
Gillard, Julia 91
Gorton, John 40n1
Greenblatt, Stephen 96, 97, 101
Greer, Germaine: cuntpower theory 35–9; media coverage of 50–3
Guy, Camille 59n5

Hall, John 106
Hartley, John 37
Harvard Educational Review (Withorn) 65–6
Hathaway, Ann 96, 97, 99
Hawthorn, Susan 25
Hellerstein, William 70
Hemmings, Clare 83
Henderson, M. 4n2
Henry, Astrid 86–7
Hesford, Victoria 84, 91, 92n8
Hoffman, Abbie 8, 14
Huffington, Arianna *see* Stassinopoulos, Arianna
Huffington, Michael 44
Human Sexual Response (Masters and Johnson) 31

Innis, Roy 68
International Socialist Review (Reed) 11
International Women's Year (IWY) 50

Jagose, Annamarie 32
Johnson, Lesley 56
Johnston, Jill 65, 66

Jones, Margaret 38
Jones, Tony 91
Journeys gallery 89, 90

Karis, Steven 71
Keavney, Kay 57
Kempton, Sally 65
Klaslerboe, Jim 69–70
Klein, Renate 26
Koedt, Anne 28, 31–3
Korengold, Robert 15

Lake, Marilyn 37
Lapsley, John 54
Lehmann-Haupt, Christopher 64
Levine, Ben 68
The Liberated Woman and Other Americans (Decter) 58n1
Life magazine 78, 83–6, 91
Lilburn, Sandra 4n1, 59n3
The London Observer 52
Lowe, Lisa 71

McManus, Donald 1
The Madwoman's Underclothes (Greer) 40n1
Magarey, Susan 4n1, 59n3
Mahlab, Eve 54–6
Mahoney, J. Daniel 67
Mailer, Norman 8, 14–17, 63, 98
Marcuse, Herbert 33
Matthews, Jill Julius 30
Mehta, Sonny 7, 9, 11, 12
Meyer, Ann 72
Millett, Kate 15, 54, 59n4, 65, 84, 86, 91
Mitchell, Juliet 12
The Myth of the Vaginal Orgasm (Koedt) 28, 31, 33

National Advisory Committee 59n14
National Museum of Australia (NMA): exhibition at 78–82; Greer's coat 89, 90, 92n12
The National Times 38, 59n13
Neville, Richard 11
The New Chastity and Other Arguments against Women's Liberation (Decter) 58
Newsweek 15, 65
New York Stock Exchange 8
New York Times 15, 64, 97
Nice Time 11
Nolan, Sybil 37

The Observer 45
Owens, Lynn 69
Oz magazine 11, 88, 90

Paglia, Camille 104
paisley coat *see* feminist fashion icon, paisley coat
Penunuri, Sue 69

INDEX

Peters, Terry 68
Pleasure and Danger: Exploring Female Sexuality (Vance) 40n3
Plunkett, Eugenia 72
Pol magazine 39
Powell, Betty 72

Quinn, Sally 36

Radner, Hilary 92n3
Raskin, Jonah 8
The Real Matilda (Dixson) 17
record keeper 22–6
Reed, Evelyn 11, 66
Reich, Wilhelm 33
Reschke, Tricia 90
Revolution for the Hell of It (Hoffman) 8
Richards, Bea 70–1
Roiphe, Katie 97
Rorvik, David 67
Rosenbergh, Sandra 72
Rowbotham, Sheila 10
Rowlands, S. 4n2
Rubbo, Kiffy 26
Rubin, Jerry 9, 18

Scheil, Katherine 96, 100
SCREW: The Sex Review (Greer) 38
SCUM *see* Society for Cutting Up Men (SCUM)
Seattle Post-Intelligencer 65
The Second Sex (de Beauvoir) 12, 17
The Second Wave 59n7
second-wave feminism 1–3, 4n4, 25, 28–9, 32, 36, 38–9, 43–4, 56, 63–4, 66, 73–4, 91, 92n4, 98, 102, 107
Segal, Lynne 30, 33, 34
The Selling of Feminism (Dreifus) 66
Sex and Destiny: The Politics of Human Fertility (Greer) 24, 26
sexual liberation 29–31
Sexual Politics (Millett) 15, 65, 84, 85
The Sexual Revolution (Reich) 33
Shakespeare's Wife (Greer) 107; criticised for whimsical storytelling 101; detractors and positive critics of 96; Greer's literary criticism 99; invective-ridden critique of 96; love and marriage in 104–5; speculations in 100; weakest section of 106
Shakespeare, William 96, 97, 101–5, 107
Shaw, Bernard 105
Sheridan, Susan 4n1, 59n3
Smart, Carol 30
Smith, Natalie 92n3
Snitow, Ann 30
Snowdon, Lord 83
Society for Cutting Up Men (SCUM) 10
Soul on Ice (Cleaver) 15

Stassinopoulos, Arianna 43–5; competing for average woman 55–7; media coverage of 50–5; visited Australia 48–50
Steinem, Gloria 53, 72
Strumpet Voluntary 7–10
The Subversive Stitch (Parker) 88
Suck newspaper 34, 38
Summers, Anne 32, 37, 38, 53, 59n5
The Sunday Times 23
The Sun-Herald 51
Sydney Morning Herald 11
The Sydney Morning Herald 43, 44, 48, 51, 52

The Taming of the Shrew (Shakespeare) 104
Tanner, Lesley 11
Taylor, Anthea 85–6, 91
The Dick Cavett Show (TDCS) 62, 63, 73; and ABC network 67, 69; guest host of 63, 67, 74n1; letters to 64
'The White Negro' (Mailer) 14
Thompson, Jeanette 72
Time magazine 84
Tolstoy, Leo 105
The Total Woman (Morgan) 58n1
transatlantic orientation: Cleaver, Eldridge 11–15; Greer as outsider 10–11; Strumpet Voluntary 7–10; Wollstonecraft, Mary 17–18
Tynan, K. 85
The Tyranny of Structurelessness (Freeman) 47

United States: *The Female Eunuch,* published in 63; Greer's reception in 62–74; letters collected and preserved in 74
University of Melbourne Archives (UMA) 23, 25–6, 26n7

Vashti's Voice 59n8
Verstak, Tania 90, 91
Victorian Women's Liberation and Lesbian Feminist Archives (VWLLFA) 25
Village Voice 65
Vogue magazine 78, 83–6
Voices from Women's Liberation (Tanner) 11

WAA *see* Women's Action Alliance (WAA)
Wallace, Christine 2, 10, 14, 46, 102–4
Ward, Georgie 26n8
Warner, Marina 24
Weeden, Wardell N. 70
WEL *see* Women's Electoral Lobby (WEL)
Wertheim, Barbara 53–5
Western feminist theory 83
Whitehouse, Mary 59n9
The Whole Woman (Greer) 80, 91, 99, 105
Will in the World (Greenblatt) 96, 97, 101
Willis, Ellen 30

INDEX

Wilmot, John 98, 100
Withorn, Ann 65–6
WLM *see* Women's Liberation Movement (WLM)
Wollstonecraft, Mary 17–18
Woman's Day 45, 55, 56
Women's Action Alliance (WAA) 50, 59n11, 59n14
Women's Commission (1973) 38
Women's Community Aid Association 53–4
Women's Electoral Lobby (WEL) 25, 54
Women's Lib: A Second Look (Millett) 84
women's liberation 29–31
Women's Liberation Movement (WLM) 31–2, 35, 54
Women: The Longest Revolution (Mitchell) 12
Women Who Want to Be Women (WWWW) 59n11
Wright's Native Son (Richard) 12